The Contemporary

Dachshund

The World of Dogs

written and compiled by
Eileen Falconer-Douglas

t.f.h.
KINGDOM

Front Cover
Devonwood Solo Adventurer
Owned by Pauline Anderson.
Photo: Paul Anderson

Left
(*top*)
Ch Keneven Talladdale
of Willowfield
Owned by Lady Dick-Lauder.

(*middle*)
Ch Shardagang Masterplan
at Bothlyn
Owned by Elizabeth Fulton.
Photo: David Dalton

(*bottom*)
Ch Mastelli Oscaratum
Owned and bred by Vivian Stagg.

contents

(Unless it is otherwise stated, Eileen Falconer-Douglas has written the text)

Acknowledgements

The Contemporary Dachshund is the collective product of all those Dachshund enthusiasts who gave so generously of their time and expertise, with no object other than the good of the breed. Their commitment is to be applauded. As compiler, my aspiration throughout the book has been to offer something for everyone. Above all, the need was for a book that could be recommended to first-time Dachshund owners.

On behalf of all Dachshund enthusiasts, my first thanks go to the following

TFH/Kingdom Books
the publishers.

The Dachshund Club (UK)
for releasing Sayers' *Standard of Points* and Robert Cole's *Confirmation and Movement*, both of which are classics.

The Miniature Dachshund Club (UK) and its members,
who were an endless source of information.

Dr Sylvia Kershaw
for her concise history of the breed and her interesting,
no-holds-barred section on judging.

Terry Thorn
who also contributed a section on judging, sharing many of his best-kept secrets.

Betty Munt
who has 50 years in the breed and 27 champions under her belt.

Val Skinner
owner of the famous Ritterburg Standard Wires

Elizabeth Fulton (Bothlyn)
who gave us what no other Dachshund book has:
a comprehensive, step-by-step guide to stripping the Miniature Wire-haired coat.

Jeff Crawford
for his generous help, advice and encouragement

Mrs Pam Evans (Amberleigh) and Mrs Betty Cole-Hamilton (Beltrim)
for their amusing anecdotes.

Daniel Roberts, Jeff Horswell, Margaret Turner and Jim and Jean Sinclair
for the sections for newcomers to the show scene.

The Contemporary Dachshund may be my brain-child but, without the generous help of these people, I could never have assembled such a wealth of information. For this, and on behalf of all Dachshunds, I thank you.

Foreword

It has to be said that the even the most non-doggy persons among us will without doubt recognise a Dachshund when they see it. They will also know that the Dachshund's country of origin is Germany. How many other breeds, one might ask, are so easily recognisable?

Nowadays, of course, the Dachshund is universal, a citizen of the world, loved for what it is – a hardy and loyal companion. In fact, the Dachshund is a dog of such good nature and intelligence that it is a privilege to be owned by one. I say *owned by*, for such is his character. What does seem to come as a bit of a surprise to some, however, is the fact that Dachshunds come in two sizes and six varieties – one to suit every taste and circumstance.

For those seeking more information about the breed there are various books on the subject. As a Dachshund enthusiast, I have read most of them. My interest has spanned a period of almost 40 years. However, of late I have been aware that there is a need for an up-to-date book written with the new pet owner, the novice exhibitor and the more experienced breeder in mind.

Reading *The Contemporary Dachshund* I was very impressed by its fresh approach and by the concept of its co-writer, editor and compiler, Eileen Falconer-Douglas, who brought together so many acknowledged experts to share their expertise. She has compiled information, advice, anecdotes and examples from the most accomplished breeders, exhibitors and judges of our time, so the description 'Contemporary' is most apt.

The Contemporary Dachshund is already being widely spoken of in Dachshund circles, and its publication eagerly awaited. The book has something to offer everyone, from readers who wish to browse and prospective pet owners planning to acquire a Dachshund to confirmed Dachshund enthusiasts such as myself.

I have no hesitation in recommending *The Contemporary Dachshund* as an essential and valuable book on the breed.

Lovaine Coxon
(D'Arisca Dachshunds)

Introduction

Do we need another book about Dachshunds? Here I have to admit that there are some very fine books on the market. However, most of these are manuals written for people already experienced in the breed, with very few chapters intended for the complete novice.

It is so easy for experienced Dachshund people to forget those anxious days when we owned Dachshunds for the very first time, and the awful 'bloomers' we made when first putting a tentative foot in the show ring. Or, indeed, when we were wondering whether our Dachshunds had any show potential at all. Here it must be said that not all owners have to enter the highly competitive world of championship showing; great fun may still be had at local Open Shows, with the added attraction that the emphasis at these shows is fun. They are less stressful, less competitive and entirely more satisfying for the novice.

Then there were those times so easily forgotten by experienced dog owners when we were not sure how to manage the new addition to our family. The first thought that springs to mind was the desperate search for a book on the subject, only to find that most of those on offer were full of eulogies for past champions and listings of their pedigrees.The best of these books, whilst of great interest to the experienced breeder/exhibitor, are of little use to the layman. Some are more instructive than others; but what most share is a somewhat timeworn language that rarely deals with the contemporary (as in modern) Dachshund. To be fair, in some cases great care has been taken to update and revise some of the older and more valuable editions, thereby putting something of a strain on the language and complexity of the content.

For this reason it is felt that there is a need for a comprehensive book about Dachshunds, aimed at everyone from the complete novice to those more proficient in the breed. It is our intention to offer a book about Dachshunds written in the simplest terms and dealing with everyday problems. Nonetheless, however experienced one individual might be concerning Dachshunds, few can be expert in all areas. With two sizes and six varieties to choose from, there must be blind spots in all of us.

For this reason, in writing and compiling this book I have relied heavily on the wide experience of Dachshund owners from all corners of the United Kingdom. For the more experienced Dachshund owners and exhibitors, I hope that, since there is always something new to learn, this book will provide you with many hours of enjoyment, even debate. With this in mind we have included a few lighter moments, some of which will demonstrate that not even the most well-informed are infallible and that making up a champion can, and often does, have its amusing side. Perhaps it will also remind some of us that within the cut and thrust of the show circuit, and the intense rivalry that often overtakes commonsense, our Dachshunds, champions or not, remain primarily the loyal companions we take home with us at the end of the day.

With all of this in mind we offer you *The Contemporary Dachshund*, written by numerous experts – their generous and collective experience assembled in one book.

Eileen Falconer-Douglas
(Bonnerhill)

1 History

Dr Sylvia Kershaw
(By kind permission of The Dachshund Club UK)

Before the 19th century

In the past, dogs served various purposes, but were mainly used as hunting dogs, companions and pets for the ladies. Small specimens of many shapes seem to have been handed over to the women in the household for many centuries, probably for thousands of years. Among these, as illustrated on a tablet from a place near Thebes in 1500 BC and in clay models from ancient Mexico, were small, short-legged dogs which, by a violent stretch of the imagination, could be thought to be the origin of the Dachshund. While no pure breed can be traced this far back, it does show that short-legged dogs have existed for a very long time.

Going back to Roman times in this country – a mere 2000 years – and to Medieval times, large hunting dogs of rather fearsome appearance, similar to our Mastiffs, were common among the rich, and were considered suitable companions for inmates of Norman Castles. Hunting was the preoccupation of all men when they were not at war; the rich rode horses and their servants and followers went on foot.

Over the centuries, as forests were cleared in Britain and more open country developed, hunting with packs of fairly large hounds, such as Foxhounds and Wolfhounds, became traditional. Men on foot had companions such as Deerhounds, Otterhounds, Greyhounds and, much later, Beagles, all of which were of a fair size and relatively long-legged.

On the continent, deforestation was slower, and large forests still exist today, particularly in Germany and central Europe. Hunting in these forests followed a different pattern: men on horses were few, and a few large hounds, perhaps two pairs, appear to have been used. This can be seen in hunting scenes on tapestries and pictures from the late Middle Ages. Certainly, from the 16th century onwards, short-legged and rather long-bodied dogs with pendant ears were used for hunting.

Jacques de Fouilloux, in 1560, published a book called *La Veneri* which contained woodcuts of these dogs, both going to hunt and being encouraged to go to earth. These dogs appear to be very large, and I do not think that anyone would describe them as Dachshunds. I believe they were the prototypes of several short-legged hounds which developed in different counties according to their various circumstances: Basset Hounds, which came to be used in packs; Basset Griffon Vendéen; Basset Fauve de Bretagne; and others, including the Dachshund. In different countries, by selective breeding, different breeds were 'created' for different purposes, but all remained hounds, with the desire and ability to hunt, and with short legs and relatively long bodies.

In Germany and neighbouring areas there was a need for a hound small enough to get through dense undergrowth but who was also very robust, with a really good nose for hunting and tracking wounded game. Quarry such as deer and boar would take refuge in the densest part of the forest. These hounds, being small and short-legged, did not travel fast and therefore did not lose contact with the hunters, who were either on foot or on the sturdy, short-legged horses of the early continental type that travelled slowly in the forest. These hounds had to give tongue continually while hunting, as Dachshunds still do. They barked to mark the spot but did not attack, as larger and more aggressive hounds might do.

As a useful side-line, where vermin such as foxes and badgers were plentiful, a dog that was small and brave but not too aggressive was most valuable. However, it is noticeable in the accounts that the Dachshund was valued principally for its hunting and tracking skills, despite his name of Dachshund (badger dog). This is borne out in the modern working trials for Dachshunds in Germany, where as many points are given for hunting and tracking as for going to earth. In the 19th century there was confusion about the history and purpose of the Dachshund, many people thinking he should be classed as a terrier and simply used to go to earth. However, it is clear from history that the Dachshund was, and still is, a hunter.

In 1685 Paullini wrote a book in which he mentions Dachshunds by name, so they had obviously gone by that name for some time. Previously they were known as *bibarhunds* (beaver dogs); *burrow dogs*; *earth dogs*; and *badger creepers*, among other things. By the end of the 17th century they were recognised as a definite breed. De Fouilloux, in the 16th century, distinguished two varieties: *some smooth with short hair and crooked legs, and some with straight legs but wire-haired*. In 1793, Buffon shows pictures of two Dachshunds: one black-and-tan, and one mainly white, and they definitely look wire-haired. In the original woodcuts shown by de Fouilloux, the dogs being urged to go to ground have plumed tails and fringed ears, so it would seem that the long-haired variety was also known, though it was a good deal rarer than the other two types.

Von Flemming, in the early 18th century, described the dogs as *small, long and slender in body... with short legs somewhat bent... they should be called the dwarfs of all other dogs, and although they are small they are nevertheless exceedingly zealous... they crawl, drive and track their quarry, giving tongue and holding their game at bay with as much zeal and vigour as is probably exhibited by any other dog... This dwarf species is usually coloured red or black, with pendant ears and almost like a hound except for dwarfish size.*

In 1746 Dobel says: *Amongst all the dogs described this must be the smallest. Nevertheless he has to be the most courageous... I have found the best ones are the black, chocolate, or red dogs which have somewhat bent feet.*

So the Dachshund developed, affectionately called the *Dachsel* or *Dackel* – which came to be known in Germany as the *Tecklel* or *Tekel*. They were small, low to ground, short-legged, with rather pointed muzzles and pendant ears. In colour they were black with tan markings, red or chocolate. They sometimes had white patches on the throat and breast, but this was not regarded as desirable. Dapple colouring with a wall eye is described in some early records, and also a 'striped tiger', occurring rarely and greatly prized. By the end of the 18th century they were well known, used for hunting and tracking and going to earth, and recognised for their great courage and keenness. Tradition has it that they were kept in small packs of four or five by foresters, though owned by the nobility. They lived with the forester and his family in their cottages, and this background may partly account for the fact that, generally speaking, Dachshunds do best in small groups, closely associated with human beings, rather than in kennels.

The 19th century and beyond

In the 19th century the breed continued to thrive. In the 1840 German stud book for all breeds 54 Dachshunds were registered by owners who came to be regarded as famous breeders. Around 1868 perhaps the most famous of the German breeders were from the von Daake family: father, son and grandson were known for decades. In 1879 the first Standard of Points was drawn up.

When Wilhelm von Daake [the father] began to breed, his motto was: *The teckel should be bred as a hunting dog.* This remains the ideal for German breeders to this day. Von Daake's ideal weight for Dachshunds was about 7.3kg (16lb), although he admitted he found it difficult to keep weights below 9kg (20lb). Pictures of dogs of that era show them to be without an ounce of fat or superfluous flesh. Since the same may be said of Dachshunds shown on the continent of Europe at present, they may not have been much smaller than some of our dogs today.

Since Dachshunds traditionally were kept in forests by foresters although owned by the aristocracy, we are not surprised to learn that Wilhelm von Daake used to go to the forest every weekend to see his Dachshunds at work. At this time a head forester, Diezel, writes: *Dachshunds without doubt are among the most likeable of dogs. They are particularly faithful, affectionate and friendly, at the same time intelligent and teachable. In the house they are clean, and well behaved, and outside faithful, alert, and reliable watch-dogs. For the hunter the Dachshund is the undisputable companion, to some extent the universal dog.*

Von Daake seems to have concentrated on line breeding, and established perhaps one of the first real strains, his stock being easily recognised by other Dachshund breeders. He specialised in reds, and his famous stud dog, Monsieur Schneidig, was responsible for what we now call the true *Schneid* red: a glorious bright, clean colour without any black hairs. Known stud dogs appeared, notably Hundersport Waldman and Schulpfer Euskirchen, who remained rivals for top honours for some years, and who feature in the pedigree of dogs and bitches imported into the United Kingdom and the United States of America about this time.

At the same time the breeding of dapples became popular, and even whites bred from dapples. Photographic records show that several of these whites existed around 1900. Similarly, Silver Grey Teckels, bred from chocolates, were known. However, after 1895 the difficulties of breeding these colours caused them to be given up in favour of black-and-tans and reds.

The first Long-haired Dachshund appeared in a show in Hanover in 1882. This was believed to be descended from a cross between a spaniel and a Smooth-haired Dachshund.

However, it can be argued that, since Long-haired Dachshunds appear in the early woodcuts and engravings and spaniels were rare in that part of Germany, the Long-haired variety probably existed all along but was less popular. A cross with a long-haired gundog similar to the Munsterlander is another possibility.

In 1888 the *Deutscher Teckelklub* was founded and in 1890 the *Teckelstammbuch* was started – the stud book reference for all registered Dachshunds in Germany to this day. Now the Deutscher Teckelklub is a great organisation, with its own building and a staff of about eight. Gradually the rules, which now strictly govern the breeding of Dachshunds in Germany, were worked out. These rules still include trials for hunting, tracking and going to earth after the fox, as these are still believed to be an essential part of the make up of the Dachshund.

The first Dachshunds to appear in England are reputed to have been brought over by Prince Albert, the Prince Consort, in the 1840s, though there is some evidence that Queen Victoria had one in 1833. From that time it seems there were always some Dachshunds in the Royal Kennels, and there is a well-known picture of Queen Victoria with a Dachshund at her feet – some would say looking lovingly into her face, but I suspect she had a titbit in her hand! In any case, Dachshunds became popular quite rapidly, particularly among hunting and shooting men. It is said that Prince Albert shot pheasants using Dachshunds to drive the birds; and certainly, in the 1880s, Mr E Hutton said [according to Vero Shaw]: *In covert shooting they are equal to any spaniel, and superior in very thick cover.*

There was a great debate in Great Britain at this time as to whether Dachshunds were hounds or terriers. This stemmed from the mistaken idea that they were bred only to go to earth. The controversy led to some alteration of the conformation, in that the hound enthusiast tended to breed larger, heavier dogs with peaked heads, low set ears and massive bone. An engraving published in 1880 shows the terrier type to be what we think of now as the typical well-boned, normal-headed Dachshund. Some of the hound type were undoubtedly exported to the United States of America, and caused considerable criticism from those who knew the real Dachshund in Germany.

From the beginning there was a great variation in size, many being quite small. Mr Hutton became a great enthusiast, describing the dog as *big dog in small compass*. He said they were most fitted for hunting, giving tongue throughout, and possessing such extraordinary scenting powers that they *may be trained to hunt anything from a deer to a mouse and when trained, for courage and pluck are superior to any breed, will not tire easily and will follow the chase for many hours without a break.* He admitted they were obstinate but said that, once trained, they were intelligent, excellent guard and house-dogs, peaceable with their own variety, and could be kept in groups.

The first standard drawn up in England, ignoring the German one, described the head as *very houndy*, with deep flews, peaked skull, and low set ears. The topline had a marked arch over the loin, which was said to be *higher than the shoulders*. There was a marked *crook* in the front legs. The chest was broad, deep and large. Thick feet with hard pads were essential. Except for the feet, there was [from 1907] a gradual change towards the German and continental standards, to the standard today.

The Rev G F Lovell was an early enthusiastic breeder and one of the founder members of the Dachshund Club. He describes, in detail, measurements of a handsome fallow red bitch called Schlupferle, born in 1875:

Tip of nose to stop 3in
Stop to occiput 4in
(Note: this increased length would be due to peaked not flat skull)
Length of forearm 5in
Girth of pastern 3in
Height at shoulder   . . . . .12in (Hutton says ideal 8–10in)
Height at elbow 6in
Height at hock 4in
Height at loin 13in
Length of tail . . . . 11in (Hutton says ideal 9–12in)
Weight 23lb
Age . . . . .4 years 10 months.
(Note: 1in = 2.54cm and 1lb = 0.454kg)

Mr Lovell also said that the loose skin of the Dachshund was an essential part of its make-up, noting that the dog can contract the skin at will. Many Dachshund owners have discovered this for themselves when trying to pick up an unwilling dog by the scruff of the neck.

The first Dachshund to appear at a show in England (Birmingham 1870) was Mr Fisher's Feldmann, born and bred by HRH Prince Edward of Saxe-Coburg. The first to be called *Champion* (and how a dog became a champion at this time is obscure) was Dessauer, born in 1874 and bred by Count Picker of Wurtemburg. He was owned by Mrs Merrick Hoare, a lady regarded as a very successful breeder and a great authority on the breed. The second champion to be made up in England was a dog called Xaverl, owned by Mr Arkwright but born in 1876 at the Royal Kennels near Stuttgart. It is interesting to note that he had the same sire as the bitch whose measurements are given above.

The first separate class for Dachshunds was in 1873 in Great Britain and some five years later in Germany. At this time, and right up to the early part of the 20th Century, British Dachshunds were also shown, and won prizes in Germany.

Mr Arkwright, who later made his name as a great breeder of Pointers, was at this time an enthusiastic Dachshund breeder and one of the founder members of the Dachshund Club. In 1881 four gentlemen – Mr Arkwright, Major Harry Jones, Mr Montague Wootten and the Reverend G F Lovell – met at Cox's Hotel in Jermyne Street and formed the Dachshund Club, the first club in the world for Dachshund lovers and breeders. Mr Wootten became the first Secretary. These gentlemen all owned Dachshund kennels of considerable size and had bred several champions. Among others, Mr Arkwright owned Ch Maximus, whose son Ch Charkow was directly descended from Xaverl. When mated to the bitch Wagtail, bred by Mr Arkwright and owned by Major Harry Jones, Ch Charkow produced in 1886 the famous Ch Jackdaw, who won the Fifty Guinea Challenge Cup for the best Dachshund 11 times. He also gave his name to the trophy, now valued at many hundreds of pounds, and awarded as the Jackdaw Trophy to the top-winning Dachshund of the year.

In 1886 the first Dachshund Special Show, combined with Basset Hounds, was held, and almost 200 Dachshunds were entered. Top honours went to Ch Maximus, then aged five years.

It is an indication of the enthusiasm and commitment of Dachshund breeders in England that in 1898 Mr E S Woodiwiss published a list of all registered Dachshunds, complete to 31 December 1896, giving such details as sires, dams, colours, breeders and owners. Those listed numbered 2500 to 3000, and it is not only a valuable source of information about dogs of that time but also evidence of the great popularity of the breed. The publication also contains engravings and photographs of some of the champions of the day, from whom our present dogs are mainly descended. Careful study of this list shows that the top breeders tended to line breed, producing many champions by this method.

In the United States of America, William Loeffler of Millwaukee, Wisconsin was the first to show a Dachshund. He went to Germany in 1879 and bought a dog and bitch from the Duke of Coburg. Later, he bought Hundesports Bergmann, a chocolate, son of the famous Hundesports Waldmann who was winning everything in Germany at that time. Bergmann was a winner in Chicago in 1891. In 1888 Arthur Padelford bought a dog from Major Emil Ilgner, one of Germany's greatest authorities on the breed. George Semler of New York also bought from Major Ilgner and Mr Semler's East End affix became famous, exerting the greatest influence on Dachshund breeding in America at this time. Major Ilner and the equally famous Dr Fritz Engelmann judged at shows in America and Great Britain, and both wrote books about the Dachshund which are classics in this field.

There were many imports into America from both Germany and Great Britain before the First World War, mostly Smooth-haired but also occasional Long-haired and Wire-haired. However, the latter two varieties at that time were a good deal less common. At the end of the 19th century three men were the 'moving spirits' in the organisation of the Dachshund Clubs of America: Harry Peters, G Muss-Arnolt and Dr Montebacher. The first licensed show, in which 204 Dachshunds were entered, was held in the United States of America. The judge, Mrs Tainter, famous for her pre- and post-war Voewood Dachshunds, was one of those responsible for keeping the Dachshund Club of America going during the difficult war years.

After the 1914–18 war there was a surge of imports from Germany, both in the United States and Great Britain, where the breed had become very low in numbers and quality. Famous affixes such as Flottenberg, Lichtenstein and von Falltor will be found in the pedigrees of almost all American and British Dachshunds of today, if they are traced back far enough. An export from Britain to America, Ch Kensal Call Boy, was the first Dachshund to win Best In Show (BIS) in America at an all-breeds show, followed by the American-bred Ch Herman Rinkton (a lovely dog, going by his photograph) who won 14 BISs. Other outstanding breeders at this time were the van Courts in California with their White Gables affix; the Mehrers in Long Island with their von Marienlust affix; and Lawrence Horswell, who judged and taught about Dachshunds and is still an authority to be consulted by all Dachshund lovers. What a privilege it must have been to hear him during one of his ringside discussions on type, construction and gait. Much of his work is behind Rachael Page-Elliot's book and the film *Dogsteps*, and is increasingly relevant today.

In Great Britain at about the same time, John Sayer wrote *The Illustrated Standards of Points of the Dachshund*, the 'bible' of Dachshund breeders throughout the English-speaking world.

Recent history

The early history of the Long-haired Dachshund is more obscure than that of the Smooth although, as has already been said, it seems from an early woodcut that they existed alongside the Smooths and Wires from the early days. It is interesting that some of this breed were dappled.

In the 18th century Fischer, supported by later research, reports a thoroughbred train of Long-haired Dachshunds, known as the Wopke strain, used mainly as bird dogs and not so good below ground. It was said that the foresters kept careful records of this strain for many generations. Certainly in the 19th century Long-haired appeared in smooth litters after several generations, and these were all black-and-tan or black. The first reds came from one of these Long-haired Dachshunds crossed with one of the pure red von Daake line of Smooth Dachshunds. The first Long-haired Dachshund appeared in Britain in about 1900 but serious breeding did not start till about 1920, and in America not until 1930, when they rapidly became popular.

The Wire-haired Dachshund also appeared fairly early on in the history of the breeds, as early pictures show. It seems that the Wire-haired Pinscher was crossed with a Smooth Dachshund in the early days, leading to a dog much higher in the leg and lacking Dachshund type. Later, a Dandie Dinmont was imported into Germany and used to improve the lowness to ground but it inevitably introduced soft coat problems. At this time all coats of Dachshunds were interbred.

The Wire-haired Dachshund came to England around 1888, but it did not gain in popularity until recently. In Germany in 1938 they were the most popular variety, and have maintained their popularity to the present time. Between the two world wars there was much activity and common interest between Germany and Britain, and Germany and the United States of America. Several outstanding Smooths were imported in Britain, like Theo von Newmarkt, whose son, Remargen Max, had a great influence at stud and was said to be a great dog with an excellent Dachshund temperament. He was an ancestor of the equally great Ch Wolf von Birkenschloss who was rated Excellent at shows in Germany and rapidly became a British champion. His influence was to bring down size, many English Dachshunds being very big at this time, and to improve shoulders.

Madame Rikovsky, herself a refugee from Russia, imported Wolf, and later two other dogs of considerable importance and influence: Kunz Schneid, from the famous von Daake line of reds, and Ch Zeus von Schwarenberg, from the well-known Luitspoldsheim kennels. Nearly all our kennels producing reds go back to Kunz Schneid, and Zeus was of particular interest because he carried a gene for long hair. From Zeus descended the famous Silvae kennels of Mrs Grosvenor-Workman; and, through his grandson, Ch Womacks Rhinefields, came Cedavoch, Turlshill, Limberins, who also had lines to Kunz Schneid, and D'Arisca. For the Silvae kennels Zeus sired Ch Silvae Zebo, who in turn sired Ch Silvae Lustre, Ch Silvae Polish and later Ch Silvae Banjo. Banjo and Polish mated and produced Ch Silvae Sailors Quest. Silvae Querry, brother of Quest, went to Australia and was largely responsible for the tremendous surge in quality of the Australian Dachshund at that time.

Ch Keneven Talladale of Willowfield – a perfect example of a Schneid red. Owner: Lady Dick-Lauder

Quest sired 30 champions in the United Kingdom, among them Ch Ashdown Skipper, who also sired many Champions; Ch Urbatz v d Howitt, who was the foundation of the Rhinefield kennels; and Turlshill Pirate, who was the basis of the Turlshills and the grandsire of Ch Womack Wrightstarturn. Very many of the Womack Champions went back to Urbatz and Quest.

Among those who concentrated on the Zeus von Schwarenburg line was Alf Hague with his Limberin kennel, whose Miniatures, came down from a very small bitch of the same line and are behind some Miniature pedigrees today. He also used Heracles von Liebestraum, a dog imported from Belgium by Joan Foden and Nina Hill, who was medium in size and very sound.

Nearly all dogs in the 1990s go back in pedigree to these famous dogs and kennels, and the most successful have several lines to the same dog.

In Long-hairs, Ch Zeus von Schwarenberg's son, Ch Limberin Lounge Lizard, mated with a Zeus daughter and produced Long-haired Ch Clonyard Corky. In 1928 a bitch in whelp from

Ch Golden Patch, an early Long-hair. Photo: Ralph Crawford

the von Fels kennels in Germany was imported, and produced Ch Rose of Armadale and Ch Rufus of Armadale; later, in 1930, Otter von Fels was imported. From these two lines came the von Walder and Primrosepatch kennels, which produced many champions. Ch Silvae Lustre (smooth, and grandson of Zeus) mated with a bitch descended from Ch Rufus of Armadale. This produced Imber Black Coffee; from him came Ch Albaney Red Rheinhart, Ch Phaeland Phreeranger, Ch Imber Hot Coffee, Ch Imber Coffee Bean, Ch Imber Cafe au Lait and Ch Kennhaven Caesar (who was behind the Swansford kennels and such dogs as Ch Voryn Café au Lait).

Although the well-known Woolsack was exhibited in 1888, little progress was made with Wire-hairs until the 1920s and 1930s. During and after the 1914-1918 war, many of the best Wire-hairs in Germany were sent to Sweden and from there, after the war, to Great Britain and America. From these early imports Mrs M Howard founded her Seale kennels. Mrs Blandy bred Ch Achsel, who was highly praised by Major Emil Ilgner, who was possibly then the most famous Dachshund breeder and judge in the world. Aschel sired many champions, and eventually went to America where he sired many more. In 1937 Wisden Sports Pimavera was imported from Sweden, and when, after the 1939-1945 war, breeding started up again, the Grunwald kennels of Wires hung onto this Sports line. From them came Ch Gisbourne Inca and, later, Ch Mordax Music Master, both owned by Mrs Farrand. These two dogs are behind nearly all our present Wires. From the same lines came the Silvae Wire-hairs and a succession of Wire-haired champions.

Ch Primrosepatch Jasper.

Miniatures only came on the scene in England in the 1920s although, in Germany, little ones appeared regularly, and were interbred. In 1925, Dr Mary Blakiston and Miss New imported a Miniature Smooth dog and the following year a bitch. In 1929, Miss Dixon imported a bitch in whelp from Germany. From these imports are descended all our Miniature Smooths. However, added to these were several very small bitches bred in 'Standard' litters, notably Limberin, Booth, and Montreux. Miniature Long-haired dogs were also used to improve bone, head, and lowness to ground.

Miniature Long-haired dogs were imported in 1935, and produced a little dog, Knowlton Chocolate Soldier, who made a great name for himself and was the foundation of the Robsvarl and Primrosepatch [Miniature] lines.

Miniature Wire-haired dogs did not really get started until after the Second World War. Air Vice-Marshal Sir Charles Lamb bred from a small Wire bitch that was mated to a Smooth, Aggi, from whom came the dapple Huntersbroad Graphite, who was used widely at stud. Mrs Molony also imported Barro, from whom came Orkneyingas and Peredurs (Ch Peredur

Ch Voryn Café au Lait.

Exhibitors at a show in 1981.

Some eminent breeders, 1978: (left to right) Margaret Turner (Marictur), Edna Cooper (Sontag), Margaret Brown (Sowlon), Eileen Wood (Woodric) and Lawrence Brown, Margaret's son.

Pimento), and from them the Silvae Miniature Wires. From Pimento came the well-known run of Silvae 'Mouse' Champions, from one of which are descended the successful Drakesleat Miniature Wires. Another famous Miniature Wire was Ch Selwood Dittany (also sired by a Peredur dog), and from him came a succession of winners.

Separate registers were set up by The Kennel Club in 1948, creating six Dachshund breeds. The United Kingdom probably has the best Miniatures in the world, largely because, in the United Kingdom, Miniatures are weighed in the ring, so size has been controlled; this is not done in the United States, Australia, or the rest of the world. Interbreeding between coats and sizes has not been allowed in the United Kingdom since the 1970s.

In recent years there have been several outstanding Miniature Smooth dogs: Ch Limberin Americano, Ch Dandy Dan of Wendlitt, Ch Prince Albert of Wendlitt, Ch Pipersvale Pina Colada and Ch Wingcrest Smart Alec. All have produced a succession of winners. The Montreux kennel is still producing champions after 50 years.

Outstanding Miniature Wires that come to mind are the bitches Ch Sutina Barclay Charm and Ch Drakesleat Ai Jail. A study of this history brings out one important fact that faces our breeds today. Up to the Second World War, imports from Germany were made to improve stock in the United Kingdom, America, Canada and Australia. Before there were quarantine regulations, British dogs were shown with success on the Continent. Indeed, Miniature Dachshunds bred in Great Britain, both Smooths and Wires, have been shown successfully on the Continent in recent years. However, since the war, type in Germany and on the Continent has differed so much from the type bred in the rest of the world that there has been little or no interbreeding.

The Germans, having decided that they wanted the Dachshund primarily as a hunting dog, have bred them much smaller, slighter in body, with longer legs and less bone. Their temperaments have become sharper and more aggressive. The ability to take part in field trials, to track and to 'go to earth' (actually, a succession of pipes or tunnels) for live foxes is more important to them than anything else. Breeding is controlled strictly and only approved dogs can have their offspring registered. I suppose one can compare their attitude to the British attitude toward Foxhounds: the dogs are kept primarily to hunt, and seldom become companions or pets. The size is regulated by measurement just behind the forelegs, the measure being drawn very tight. The three sizes (*Standard*, *Zwerg* and *Kaninchenteckel*) have an exact limit in centimetres, and this naturally leads to a much shallower body than we expect to see.

I think it is true that in Great Britain, the United States of America and elsewhere our Standard Dachshunds have become too big and are often shown too fat. On the Continent all dogs are shown very lean – rather on the thin side. However, size has always been a problem. The old saying that *it is easier to breed a good big one than a good little one* still holds true. There were very big ones early this century, between the wars, and now. Often they are of excellent quality, but big and, if shown fat, they look bigger than ever. Having looked at the photographs and engravings of dogs that lived at the end of the 19th Century and the beginning of this century, I think that our present type is much more like those. The lowness

Standard Smooths Ch Marictur Easter Minstrel and Ch Marictur Easter Magic:
a brother and sister bred by Margaret Turner.

to ground, heavy bone and large thick feet are much more like our present type than the German one. The imports from Germany in the 1930s were regarded as excellent there and here; now they are different. We like our Dachshunds to be family pets and companions, and have encouraged a gentler, perhaps softer, temperament; but I cannot help thinking back to the foresters, who found them friendly, amiable and able to live happily in small packs. Still, all the Dachshunds I know (some more than others) will hunt, track and kill, given the chance; so, despite everything, they have not lost their natural abilities.

2 Buying a puppy

First and foremost, there should be no rush when you decide to buy a puppy. This rule applies to any breed of dog. Also,we must know what to expect.

The Dachshund temperament

We should recognise that the Dachshund is a hound, with all the traits and instincts of a hound. A Dachshund is tough, independent, arrogant and stubborn, tremendously loyal, and a strong and instinctive hunter. What a Dachshund is *not* is a lap-dog.

What kind of Dachshund?

Before buying a Dachshund puppy you should consider exactly what kind of Dachshund is best suited to your needs. In other words, what does the breed offer?

There are two sizes and six varieties of Dachshunds. In both sizes, Standard and Miniature, there are three different coats to choose from: Long-haired, Smooth-haired, and Wire-haired.

The Smooth: Ch Marictur Mr Moto, bred by Margaret Turner, owned by Sue Hunt.

The Long: Ch Kastelli Oscaratum, bred and owned by Vivian Stagg.

The Wire: Ch Bothlyn Blue Grass, bred and owned by Elizabeth Fulton.

Dr Sylvia Kershaw (right) and a Hobbithill litter at home with friends.

Head study of Jack (Bothlyn Magician). Photo: Animal Pix

Standard

The Standard Dachshund is larger than the Miniature, and the Breed Standard compiled by The Kennel Club in the United Kingdom states that the ideal weight of a Standard Dachshund is 9-12 kg (20-26lb).

It is interesting to note that many today are well over this ideal weight and, as Dr Kershaw mentioned in Chapter 1, this is probably because the Standard is not weighed when shown in the ring. Whether this is a good thing is a matter of opinion. Considering that all Dachshunds were bred for hunting and going to earth, one might be forgiven for wondering if the breeding of such large animals is practical when few of these large Dachshunds could be used as working hounds, which is the purpose for which they were originally bred.

There can be nothing sadder than a fat Dachshund, whether Standard or Miniature. All Dachshunds should move freely, the drive coming from behind. An overweight dog who lumbers along, plodding one foot in front of the other and with no natural joy to its movement, reflects bad management and an over indulgent owner.

A dapple Long-hair.

Weight is relative to bone size. What looks good on one dog can look frightful on another. There are individual Dachshunds who are obviously over the ideal weight but, where bone is relative to size, they may not actually be considered overweight. Many such animals have gained their crowns and are worthy champions.

Miniature

The Miniature varieties are strictly monitored. These little animals are weighed before showing, and bumping the scales is very much frowned upon. No Miniature Dachshund can expect to win a prize in the show ring if it is over 5kg (11lb), and this is one of the main reasons why breeders of Miniatures run puppies on. A puppy who is liable to reach a maximum weight of 5kg, possibly a few grammes over, must be thought about very carefully. While such a Dachshund will make an ideal pet, the continual weighing of its food with one eye on the scales is a frustrating business when the dog is being shown. For this reason, the breeder will often let the puppy go to a good pet home. The Kennel Club Breed Standard clearly states that the ideal weight for a Miniature Dachshund is 4.5kg (10lb).

The type or variety you choose will undoubtedly be influenced by personal preference and circumstances. With this in mind, you are well advised to study the fully-grown dog before coming to a final decision.

Where to buy

There are, of course, those very nice people up the street who own a very nice bitch and intend breeding a litter from her, just the once. If you are looking for a pet rather than a show animal you may well strike lucky here. Undoubtedly, such a purchase will be easier on your pocket. What you will not get is experienced back-up. With the best will in the world, these very nice people may have taken their darling to a top-flight dog at public stud. Unfortunately, as often happens through lack of experience and knowledge of the breed, faults may be doubled up. The resulting puppy may inherit some of the finer points from his sire, but this does not necessarily mean that, in its turn, your puppy will pass these qualities onto its own progeny. At best, pet breeders, however well-intentioned, are gambling on long odds.

Most reputable breeders are show enthusiasts who choose their stock with an eye to improving the breed. In most cases these breeders have spent years developing a particular line and are justifiably proud of the offspring carrying their affix. You can meet these people at most Kennel Club registered dog shows. All local areas have their share of open shows, while championship and breed shows are usually within a reasonable driving distance. All shows are advertised in advance in the two main, weekly canine papers: Dog World and Our Dogs. For a small entry fee you can watch the finest animals in the breed strutting their stuff around the ring. You might also consider buying a show catalogue, in which will be listed the names of the dogs being shown, with their dams and sires, dates of birth, owners and breeders – a wealth of information for a very small price. It is also interesting that the names and addresses of all exhibitors are printed in the back of the catalogue. Also, most catalogues carry advertisements, and many breeders advertise this way. Although most have lengthy waiting lists; but there should be no rush – a good dog is well worth waiting for.

The other avenues you might try are the Secretaries of Dachshund Breed Clubs. A telephone call will give you the name of anyone in your area with a litter. Also, you can obtain a list of breeders with puppies for sale from The Kennel Club. Last, but by no means least, you might consider re-homing a dog, not necessarily a puppy, from one of the Dachshund Rescue Services. These become available for all sorts of reasons: the death or illness of an owner or an elderly owner who can no longer cope, for instance. Few Dachshunds are passed on through neglect, and all animals are strictly vetted before being found a new home. These dogs are matched carefully to their new owners, the needs of the Dachshund being given top priority

A litter of Wires with four-year-old playmate, Gillian.

When to buy

No puppy should be considered until it is at least eight weeks old, and in some cases, much older.

Sometimes breeders *run on* litters. This simply means that the puppies are kept until they have developed enough for the breeder to decide what to keep, and what to let go. This often happens when the breeder is also an exhibitor in the show ring, and it does not mean that you are being offered a second-rate puppy – quite the opposite. It probably means that all the puppies have show potential.

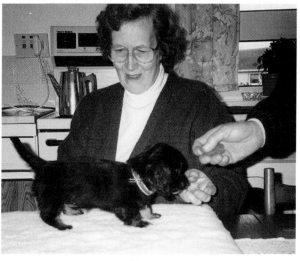

Betty Cole-Hamilton assessing potential.

Eight to twelve weeks is a critical period in the life of any puppy. No longer dependent on the dam for food, cleaning and warmth, the puppy is now free to form new attachments. It naturally takes to exploring places beyond the whelping area. Life becomes a series of exciting games, such as nipping mother and litter-mates and chewing and tasting all manner of things, from chair legs to carpets. The pup also starts the instinctive game of asserting itself in the pecking order, which inevitably leads to minor squabbles with its peers. This does not mean it is aggressive; all dogs are programmed to do this. It follows that, the sooner the puppy is settled into its new environment, with its new owner and family, the better.

Which to buy

The puppy to consider favourably is not always the largest, although size is a good indication of the quality of the litter. Uniformity is certainly smiled upon because, ideally, the puppies should all look like peas from the same pod. Unfortunately, this is not an ideal world and it is almost inevitable that there will be a 'big boy' and a 'little lad'. All being equal, it is probably wiser to opt for the average-sized puppy.

What is important is temperament. There are long-running arguments on whether genetics or

'Follow my leader.' By the time they are ready for inspection, all pups have distinct characters.

Dr Sylvia Kershaw assessing a potential 'show girl'. Not even an expert can know for sure whether she'll make it.

good management are responsible for developing good temperament. I would say that both should be considered. Research shows that nervousness can be hereditary, as can aggression. On the other hand, however fine the genealogy, a socially-deprived puppy is at a disadvantage and can develop into a nervous and fearful animal through no fault of its own. For this reason, it is important for the prospective buyer to see the environment in which the puppy has been reared.

The early weeks are so important. Stroking, talking, handling and general encouragement is vital. The most critical period in a puppy's development is from three weeks onwards, when the puppy becomes less dependent on its mother and more reliant on human beings. The puppy that scrambles out of its box and eagerly rushes to meet you, wagging its tail for attention, is almost always the most socially adaptable.

Not all puppies are exposed to the same early human contact, some may need more time to adjust. From puppies born and reared in outside kennels you must not expect too much too soon. Such puppies are unused to general household noises. Television and radio are alien to them, as are the clattering of cutlery and loud voices, even children at play. It is a new world, one they must investigate slowly.

Don't be afraid to ask questions of the breeder – and expect to be asked questions in return. The breeder will want some assurances before entrusting a puppy to your care.

If possible ask to see the parents of the puppy, as this should give you some idea what your puppy will grow into. Remember that, while the dam (mother) will usually be on hand, the sire (father) may be owned by someone else. If you are uncertain about identifying a sound and healthy puppy, ask someone with more experience to accompany you, bearing in mind that the ultimate choice must be yours and the wisest among us are not infallible.

Overall, the puppy must be clean, and you must not listen to any excuses about temporary ailments. The nose must be free from any discharge and the coat clean and in no way scurvy. The eyes should be clear, alert and bright: again, no discharge. The puppy must be clean smelling, with no indications of diarrhoea, and there must be no urine staining. The general feel of the puppy is a good indication, it must feel heavy for its size and nicely rounded. Its ribs should not be prominent, and its underline should not appear pot-bellied when it walks.

If possible make an appointment to see the puppy between feeds, requesting to be present when it is fed, to be assured that it has a normal appetite. Greedy eating is normal. Check the puppy's ears; they must be clean and without any black or tar-like substances. When you sniff them they should be sweet smelling.

Look around you, and be sure that none of the other dogs on the premises is coughing. Disregard any excuses of allergies, sore throats or splinters from stick or bones. Be very wary of the breeder who attempts to hand you a puppy, on the doorstep, so to speak. Ask to see his or her set-up. Watch carefully for the level of compatibility between the breeder and the other dogs; Dachshunds, more than any other breed, speak for themselves. If you are in any doubt, but still intend buying a puppy, ask for a certificate signed by a veterinary surgeon assuring you that the puppy and its companions are sound and in good health.

Never buy a puppy because you feel sorry for it, hard as this might sound. Hopefully, your companion will be with you for 10–16 years. A sick or disabled animal is the responsibility of the breeder and such animals can be a constant source of worry and expense.

Settling in

Settling in a new puppy might not be a problem for an experienced handler but, for the less knowledgeable, it can be a time fraught with all manner of anxieties for new owner and puppy alike. Perhaps a useful guideline would be to treat your puppy in much the same way as you might a baby: regular feeding times, a carefully balanced diet, warmth and undisturbed sleep. Between feeding and sleeping is the time for playing, initial training and socialising; not when the puppy is having 40 winks.

Name

Give your dog a name, something short and distinctive, and always call it by name. The house name need have no reflection on your puppy's registered Kennel Club name. For example, Rumpelstiltskin is fine: Rum or Rummy is better.

A litter of Smooths with Mum: always view the puppies with their dam if possible.

The bed

It is important that the new puppy has its own space to which it can retreat if necessary. It is not necessary to provide elaborate sleeping quarters; puppies are notorious chewers, particularly when they are teething. A solid cardboard box cut down is ideal. Three sides should be high enough to afford your puppy protection from draughts and the cardboard itself is excellent insulation against the cold. It has the added bonus of being disposable when dirty.

When the time comes for your puppy to have a more permanent bed there are plenty on the market to chose from. There are traditional cane baskets, padded igloos or plastic or wooden crates. Whatever your pocket allows, it must be comfortable, big enough for the dog to stretch out and be easy to clean and disinfect.

House training

House training and socialising should begin from day one, but do be reasonable. You are not in a do-or-die situation and there will be many a slip before the puppy fully understands what is expected. If you consider that it takes a human baby six months to say Da-da and a further six before it's out of nappies you might get a better perspective on things.

Toilet training should become a part of your puppy's daily routine. Encourage your pup to newspaper and take it outside as soon as it wakes up and after each feed. Don't put the dog out – go with it. At no time should the puppy be physically chastised for accidents, other than by a disapproving growl in the throat. Smacking and nose-rubbing defeats the purpose. Your puppy will want to please you; allow it the dignity it deserves. A puppy can rarely go all night without puddling on the floor until at least four or five months. Its bladder is very small, so wall-to-wall carpeting is not a good idea in the puppy's quarters. You would be better with tiles and a permanent pail of soapy water with a dash of Domestos. If your puppy can go all night, that's fine - if it can't, consider it a bonus that at least it's clean through the day.

If at all possible, set aside a small area in the garden for your pup's use. If your puppy has urinated on a small piece of carpet such as a doormat, consider laying this in its area. All dogs, whatever their breed, tend to urinate in the same place, as urine marks their territory.

Lead training

One of the first things you must introduce to your dog is its collar. This should be something light: cat collars are useful, particularly with Miniatures. Once your puppy is used to wearing a collar, and forgets it's wearing it, the time has arrived to try the lead. Again, let your puppy get used to the feel of the lead first; there must be no tugging or scolding, but plenty of praise when your pup starts walking in the right direction. If you have an older dog it is useful to walk them together. They will soon become walking pals and try to out-stride each other.

Soon your puppy will associate the sound of the lead with a walk. This is when you should start more serious training, such as teaching it to walk on your left side. A short jerk of the lead and a warning growl will discourage the pup from pulling. If it ignores the warning a sharp tug and the use of a trigger word like Side or Heel should tell your dog you are not best pleased.

'Oops!' Six-week-old Sophie does it *her* way.
When house training, don't expect too much too quickly.

Transfer of ownership

All pedigree litters should be registered by the breeder with The Kennel Club. Each puppy will then have a registered name exclusive to that dog. Most breeders have an affix, but it is not necessary to have an affix to register a litter. An affix is a word which, upon application to The Kennel Club, is granted to and reserved for the sole use of the affix holder.

With the puppy you should have received the following paperwork:

- The Transfer of Ownership correctly signed and made out to the new owner.
- A receipt of purchase.
- The Pedigree correctly made up and signed by the breeder as correct.
- A feeding chart and advice about the care and grooming of the puppy.
- Any medical history including injections, dates for worming and known allergies (if any).

A healthy, sound puppy should have been wormed at least twice, be free from fleas or any disease, and should be able to eat and drink independently of the dam.

It should be understood that all owners of Kennel Club registered dogs accept the jurisdiction of The Kennel Club and therefore undertake to abide by the general code of ethics. A copy of this code should be provided when selling or transferring a dog. Failing this, a copy can be obtained direct from The Kennel Club direct, as can an official three generation pedigree.

3 Care and management

The nicest thing about Dachshund people is their love for their animals. Even those who exhibit at the highest level tend to treat their Dachshunds as pets. Therefore you may not be surprised to learn that there is little difference in the care of a pet Dachshund and of one intended for a show career.

Talking with a very prestigious breeder and exhibitor in Wire-hairs last week, I was amused, but certainly not surprised, when she said, 'I love him so much I could eat him!' She was not displaying carnivorous yearnings; she was merely trying to express the depth of her feelings.

Best of friends: (left) Bonnerhill Esprit d'Amour (Topsy) and (right) Bonnerhill De-A-Nis (Tinker).

Even so, few pets are adorable if their care and management have been neglected. Like many breeders I very often take back and kennel Dachshunds I have bred while the dogs' owners go on holiday. It is frustrating to have a Dachshund I have bred with care and foresight returned, only to discover that, through no fault of its own, the dog has become an absolute pest.

Socialisation

Having made certain that you have purchased a fine, healthy puppy, your next task will be to socialise it. While it is true that your dog is not a human being, it should be made to understand clearly that, since it must live compatibly in a human world, there are some things it may and may not do. Your Dachshund will want to please you, and compatibility means you must live in complete accord. It follows that you must have respect for each other.

Barking

Let us start with incessant barking. All Dachshunds worth their salt bark at strangers, particularly strangers encroaching on their territory; for this reason, they make very fine watch dogs. However, from a very early age your Dachshund must be taught to stop when commanded. An excitable puppy who ignores the command must be treated firmly. It should be reassured, and then discouraged with a very firm 'No!'. If it persists when the visitor is seated, repeat the the command, placing the flat of the palm between the visitor and the dog's muzzle so that the dog cannot jump past the hand. While the dog is still barking it should not be petted, but ignored – Dachshunds hate being ignored. Give the dog five minutes and then, if it has not settled down, pick it up without a fuss and put it in another room for half an hour. You may have to repeat this procedure several times, but Dachshunds are very intelligent (albeit stubborn).

Unfortunately, this problem can be tackled in a variety of ineffectual ways by the new owner. One is to pick up the dog, laughingly telling it and the visitor that it's 'Naughty'. This confuses the dog: the voice is giving no indication that it is doing anything wrong. Equally confusing is to sweep the dog up, giving it a hard slap on the rump, and shove it into another room to be forgotten for the entire visit. The dog will undoubtedly become bored, and will probably puddle or worse on the floor. In distress, it will look for something to do – like tearing up the place. Neither of these reactions solve the problem long term. The usual result from the last example is an animal who urinates when approached, slinks belly-down on the floor, cowers in a corner or simply scoots off behind a chair, refusing to budge.

Inherent problems

Many dogs are badly-behaved because of bad management, but there are exceptions to the rule; animals who have inherited temperaments that are less than ideal. Even here, sensible handling can help with most of the distressing symptoms.

'This smells good!'

Mutual respect and affection between girl and dog.

Inherent problems are yet another reason why prospective owners should consider together the backgrounds and pedigrees of the dogs they may wish to breed from later.

It is not surprising that most breeders make some reference to temperament when advertising. Responsible breeders spend a great deal of time and effort when breeding to a certain line, and this takes years of experience. Newcomers to the breed are often impressed when a particular dog or affix is mentioned and the breeder is able to quote chapter and verse on the dog. In consideration of this expertise, have a care when passing on the blame for your own bad management. Reputable breeders will almost certainly be able to prove hitherto good temperament in dogs carrying their affixes. Your dog may be a one off – but that is doubtful.

Unfortunately, there are animals who are genetically shy and nervous. No two dogs are the same, not even litter brothers and sisters. Dogs are every bit as individual as human beings and their management must reflect this.

Young children are a frequent problem. This does not mean that no children should own pets – perish the thought! But all children should be under constant supervision when handling young dogs. A child must be educated in the needs of a small animal. As the mother of a large family, I consider there is nothing more character building than a relationship based on mutual respect between a child and a dog, and a well-adjusted child who has been taught to value all living things grows up with obvious advantages.

Aggression

Let us consider aggression. Fear aggression is a defence mechanism. A frightened dog shows aggression as a warning. This being so, it is your job to build in the dog a sense of confidence. However, an owner showing too much sympathy may very well reinforce this behaviour, confirming to the dog that it is doing the right thing. We must therefore be careful not to respond in such a manner that the dog thinks he has a reason to be afraid. It is not necessarily a stupid puppy who shows signs of fear. Quite the opposite; the more intelligent puppy will be less inclined to put itself in a position where it may get hurt and is quite capable of anticipating the outcome. This fearful state is what is known as *fear aggression*.

Fear aggression may develop as the young dog matures and, according to the response it gets from such behaviour, the dog may then start using threatening tactics for all those situations it cannot cope with. Later, as the dog matures, it will revert to this behaviour for almost every situation, such as being disturbed when eating, being put outside to relieve itself when it is raining or cold, or being moved from its favourite place in front of the fire. It may also display signs of aggression when

Dog and cat!

approached by strangers and other dogs. This state of affairs is not helped by the owner who shows equal hysteria, whether by voice or the use of a weapon such as a walking stick, as this endorses the behaviour with a mark of approval. This does not mean that we must not protect our dogs, but that it is our general attitude when dealing with these problems which most influences our dogs. Again, common sense must prevail. Probably we have all seen those owners who immediately scoop up their dogs, hugging them close and using that tone of voice which is heavily laced with hysteria. Little wonder that a young animal recognises danger long before there is reason to fear it. The combination of a 'no-nonsense' approach and the quiet removal of the dog from potentially dangerous situations is preferable by far.

Nervousness

It is understandable that puppies that have been reared in outside quarters may not be as quickly adaptable as those reared in the house. The new owners are strangers, people are a novelty and everything about this new environment is strange. Under these conditions a new puppy may well show fearful tendencies. Such a puppy must be handled with great patience. Ignore the fear, thus avoiding the temptation to reinforce it. Adopt a 'no-fuss' attitude with plenty of encouragement. Try introducing the puppy to other animals in the home and encourage it to accept them as friends. Allow relatives who are strangers to the puppy to handle it. Do not encourage the pup to sit on your knee, giving it the opportunity to hide behind you. Place it firmly on the floor, talk to it, stroke it and offer a titbit when it has been particularly brave.

I was given some very sound advice on this subject from that knowledgeable judge and show enthusiast, Mrs Betty Cole-Hamilton. We had purchased a beautiful puppy, a sound little Red Miniature Smooth-haired dog. Through no fault whatsoever of the breeder, the unthinkable happened; one week after we brought him home he became dreadfully ill. He suffered from a mysterious virus that bamboozled even our vet. After intensive care, many frightening visits to the vet's clinic and numerous injections, he recovered. However, as a 10-week-old puppy he was traumatised by the experience: our little extrovert had became a fearful little creature we hardly recognised.

Betty's advice was to ignore the situation and speak comfortingly but normally to him. All relatives and strangers were to ignore him and not show any interest in him unless he approached them first. When he did, they were to praise him without picking him up and offer him a titbit as a reward.

Happily, it worked. At 12 weeks old, Henry was returned to the veterinary centre, where he underwent his normal injections without a murmur. At 14 weeks, he was playing with his new house friends, running about the garden, being extremely naughty and eagerly meeting strangers. He had regained his appetite and put back all the weight he had lost.

The voice
It is a well known fact that all Dachshund want to please those they love and respect, and that the voice is mightier than the stick. A growl of disapproval is more impressive than a confusing slap. Neither should we shake a puppy or rub its nose in urine if it has had an accident 10 minutes ago – something it will have completely forgotten by the time you discover it. If you catch your pup in the act you can express your disapproval with a deep growl, followed by picking him up and taking him outside. If he then performs the task, great – let him know how thoroughly pleased you are with him. House training a young dog takes patience and time. If you have neither, settle for a hamster.

It is always useful to accustom your dog to the sound of your voice, with all its inflections, keeping up a running dialogue instead of ignoring its presence simply because it can't answer back. I find that talking to a dog in an everyday fashion is essential. A very young dog often finds the sound of a low-playing radio comforting. It is the tone of voice rather than the substance of the conversation that matters, although it has been estimated that a dog can learn the sound of up to 200 words in his lifetime: such distinctive sounding words as *Out* with the emphasis on the *t*, *Walk*, *Down* and *Bed*.

There can be no doubt that sound is important. The rattle of a lead and the tinkle of a spoon against a feeding bowl mean something to a Dachshund. I have a small bitch who goes wild when she hears the sound of money being rattled. She has learned (and here I confess that I do not always practise what I preach) that the sound means a treat from the local ice-cream van.

Everyday domestic sounds such as the washing machine and the vacuum cleaner soon become the norm if you don't make an issue of them. Introduce them gradually and without fuss.

General management

Your aim should be for a bright, alert and lively dog, full of energy and fun. Much of his condition will be reflected in his coat. This is usually more distinctive in the Smooth-haired varieties. In the Smooth, the coat should have a hard and bright waxy look to it. It should not be dusty or scurvy looking. The eyes should be bright, alert, intelligent and interested in all that is going on. As annoying as it sometimes is, a Dachshund who has no interest in barking at the postman is in big trouble.

Few Dachshunds are content to laze about all day. They are rarely still, unless sleeping or tired out from too much exercise. They should be bright and inquisitive. This takes energy, which you must provide by way of a balanced diet.

Mental stimulation comes naturally when Dachshunds are allowed the run of the garden: birds, next door's cat, people passing the gate, or simply digging up the flower bed. Two dogs means twice as much stimulation.

For Dachshunds kept purely as pets, grooming and general care is simpler. Even here, a well-groomed and mentally alert Dachshund, in prime condition, is an animal to be proud of.

Accommodation

Where several Dachshunds are kept it may be advisable for them sleep in outside quarters. Dachshunds need human companionship, but a balance should be considered; part house-reared and part kennelled.

Little and Large.

Companionship

Dachshunds are hounds, and hounds are pack animals. They are not, and were not bred to be, solitary animals, so you must consider whether you are capable of giving your dog the companionship it needs. No Dachshund should be left for long periods on its own, and a household where both partners work and are absent all day should not own a Dachshund.

Dachshunds are pack animals, so they need companionship.

This is why most breeders vet new owners very carefully, and it is one of the first questions asked of the prospective new owner. Leaving a Dachshund alone for extended periods is akin to leaving a small child.

For reasonable periods of absence (and we must all leave our dogs sometimes) a second Dachshund is the ideal solution. Dachshunds often need the extra stimulation of a canine friend. A second Dachshund will learn such lessons as house training from its house-mate, they will sleep together quite happily, and foraging in the garden becomes an endless game.

When you choose a companion it is wiser to consider a Dachshund of the same gender and size, though not necessarily the same variety. Standard and Miniatures together are not a good idea. The larger dog soon learns that its size is an advantage when establishing the pecking order. Few Dachshunds are intentionally rough, but size gives the larger dog an unfair advantage.

Keeping a dog and a bitch together is problematic when the bitch comes into season. Of course, if you intend to breed, and have the necessary facilities for keeping them apart at such times if necessary, then that's a different matter.

Diet

The condition of your dog must start with a balanced diet and plenty of exercise. If we believe the maxim that we are what we eat, then the same must apply to your dog. It is not enough to fill it with scraps from the table. A dog in first class condition is not produced overnight; it cannot be bathed for a special occasion and emerge faultless.

One of the telling indications of the condition of your dog is the formation of muscle. As the dog becomes more mature so its muscles develop, but a dog whose exercise is restricted cannot use its surplus energy and soon becomes obese and lethargic. Carrying too much weight can turn a relatively young dog into a middle-aged animal, at least in appearance.

There are people who advocate that young dogs should be fed to capacity. I do not subscribe to this. A young puppy should certainly be rounded and plump and feel heavy in comparison to its size but, as it reaches the five to six month stage, its diet should be steadied to suit its frame. Good, wholesome, quality food is preferable to heavy, stodgy meals. It should be quality as opposed to quantity.

The practice of over-feeding a young dog stretches its gut until, at a later age, it becomes continuously hungry. When this happens it is almost impossible to satisfy the dog. Weight then inevitably settles over the neck and shoulders, and this is the hardest fat to disperse. Such weight also puts a strain on the dog's joints, impeding its movement and throwing its elbows out.

A Dachshund should be well covered; that is to say, there should be a depth between bone and skin. If each rib is prominent when your Dachshund is lying on its side, it is certainly too thin; if you have to dig with your fingers to find the ribs, it is too fat.

Exercise

The Dachshund has become one of the most popular breeds in Britain. Bloodstock from this country has been exported as far afield as the United States, Canada, South Africa, Australia and the Far East, to name but a few. Perhaps this popularity has not done its image much good, especially that of the Miniature varieties.

Being an intelligent animal, the Dachshund naturally enjoys the high life, sleeping in its owner's bed and basking in front of the fire, and its size allows this. However, it should be remembered that no Dachshund, including the Miniature, is a lap dog, and it should not be treated as such. Such a lifestyle can knock years off a Dachshund's life, which rather defeats the argument that love and pampering express the owner's depth of feeling for the dog.

'Sorry – this seat's taken!'

As we have already said, Dachshunds are *Hounds*, first and foremost, and were not bred for a pampered and soft existence. We all know that this is done in the name of love, and we have all heard the disclaimers: 'He's special, I love him so much.' 'He's my baby, my family, my everything.' These are poor excuses for human indulgences that shorten a dog's life, and it must be said that such animals are rarely truly happy, content, or healthy. There are exceptions, as with all things, but the life expectancy of a soft and overweight Dachshund is from 7 to 10 years; that of a healthy and hardy dog in peak condition allowed to live a life close to the one for which it was bred is 10 to 16 years. A Dachshund's function is to hunt, to track wounded animals to ground. The Miniature is a smaller version of the Standard: small it may be, but it is still a hunter, revelling in the outdoor life.

The same can be said of puppies. Small puppies should not be restricted to ensure correct feet and tight shoulders. Moderate and sensible exercise is essential. If the dog is unsound in either of these areas, then the fault will develop sooner or later.

Common sense must prevail. No puppy, whatever its breed, should be allowed to exhaust itself. On the other hand, healthy play under supervision is most desirable. Until the puppy has developed muscle and bone in accordance with its age, care must be taken with all dogs. Walking distances should be increased gradually. Two or three 10-minute walks a day for a very young puppy is fine, gradually increasing the distance until it's a year to 18 months old – by which time it will probably out-walk you!

Undue restraint makes for a dull, lack-lustre dog, rendering it bad-tempered and stupid. It also ruins its outline, making it become heavy, lethargic and unattractive. Neither do Dachshunds do well when exposed to too much heat, which makes them lazy and dull coated.

Vaccination

All puppies should be vaccinated at the proper time. Your vet will advise you on this. Puppies should have at least two injections, some vets advising three, depending on whether you live in a rural or urban area. The first injection should not be given later than 12 weeks, and the second two weeks after that. Regular vaccination is essential and a booster should be given each year. More details are given in chapter 8.

Worming

Your vet can also tell you what kind of worming programme will suit your particular dog. All dogs must be wormed regularly according to their environment and life-style. Again, see chapter 8 for further details.

Routine grooming

Whether your dog is to be simply a companion or a companion and/or show exhibit, it will have to learn to stand still when being examined. Daily grooming will get your Dachshund used to this and, whatever its coat type, it should be brushed every day. This is a good habit to get into with all coats because it brings you into daily contact with your dog, a hands-on experience. It is surprising how many early warning signs can be detected simply by running your hands over your dog – such things as small tender areas, lumps, and pain of any kind. As we all should be aware, early diagnosis can mean the difference between life and death.

From as early as eight weeks old (earlier if you are a breeder) stand the dog on a non-slip surface and brush the coat soothingly, encouraging your puppy to stand rather than sit but not insisting if it is very young. Examine the ears, teeth and eyes. Check the paws and under the tail, running your fingers reassuringly over the body. Talk to it all the time, letting it know how beautiful it is.

A word about the conditions in which a Dachshund of any variety is reared: central heating, in fact too much artificial heat of any kind, is ruinous to the coat. Whilst a dog must not be subjected to draughts or damp conditions, the Dachshund does better in a cool environment.

Smooth-hairs: Of all the coat varieties it has to be said that the easiest to manage is the Smooth-hair, but that does not mean it should be neglected. A daily brushing to stimulate and rid the coat of all dead hair, 'top and tailing' with a little warm water to keep the nose and eyes and the anal and genital areas free from crust is about all that is needed.

If your dog appears to be scurvy, perhaps a revaluation of its diet should be considered. There are dietary oils on the market but, failing that, a teaspoon of polyunsaturated margarine or sunflower oil may be added to its food, along with a vitamin supplement such as SA37. A dog with a varied and nourishing diet should not need these for long.

Long-hairs: The daily grooming of the Long-haired Dachshund needs a little more attention, although not as much as one might suppose. They may need bathing more often than Smooths, but here the same rule applies: they should not be bathed too often.

Smooths, like this American show dog, have 'low maintenance' coats.

The long coat needs a little more attention than the smooth. This one is modelled by Jaimie (Bonnerhill Valentino at Denver), bred by E Falconer Douglas and owned by Sue Roberts.

Long-hairs should be brushed daily with a soft wire brush to rid their coats of any tangles or matting. They should also be towelled dry if wet, especially the underbelly. Attention should also be paid to the anal regions after they have defecated; if soiled, they should be washed and dried. I usually carry a few Nappy-Wipes with me for this.

Advice about bathing is given fully in chapter 9 – what's good enough for a show dog is good enough for a pet.

Overall, the only parts that really need to be trimmed are the feet. Again, the procedure is described fully in chapter 9.

Ch Tarchul Take Two enjoying the sunshine. The wire coat is the most difficult to keep tidy.

Wire-hairs: These Dachshunds also need daily grooming, with the added attention of stripping, the frequency of which varies according to coat type. This is not as hard as it may seem, but practice is the only way to succeed.

For a first time owner it is perhaps advisable to have your dog stripped professionally. The breeder will be able to steer you in the right direction if asked. It will also help to pay particular attention to photographs of Wire-hairs in this book. They should give you an idea of what to take off and what to leave on.

The way to learn is to watch the professional at work, paying particular attention to how he or she takes off the top coat. The most professional method is finger and thumb stripping, although, for pets, this is often done with a stripping knife and clippers.

Two nice puppies on their first venture out: Hobbithill Moorhen and Hobbithill Melanitta.

A small note might be useful here if you have not already purchased your puppy. When assessing a litter of very young Wire-haired puppies, the one to consider should be the puppy who looks almost like a Smooth-haired. This is usually the puppy most likely to develop the more correct coat as he matures.

Ears: In all sizes and varieties, ears are easily forgotten, and they shouldn't be. At least once a week the inside of the leathers should be cleaned with a little baby or almond oil to take off any of the waxy secretions naturally produced. Neglected ears can lead to all kinds of infections, especially for Dachshunds living in rural areas where the dog is more likely to come into contact with grass mites and small insects. As a deterrent you might find it useful to use an over-the-counter brand of ear drops, something mild like Johnstons or Shirleys.

Teeth: Particular attention should be paid to the mouth and teeth. Inflammatory gum disease and the accumulation of plaque are progressive problems. Few dogs like having their mouths inspected, but constant attention does help them to become accustomed to it.

Chewing helps to prevent a build-up of tartar, but never give your dog poultry or rabbit bones. It is not the size of the bones that causes the problem, but their brittleness and tendency to break into dangerous splinters. You might consider large marrow bones or specially treated bones from the pet shop, and there are some excellent proprietary brands of chews on the market. The Nylabone company produces an excellent range of chews and toys that help keep the teeth clean as the dog plays with them by breaking down the deposits of tartar. Softer bones are not ideal; they tend to grind down into abrasive matter and can irritate the lining of the bowels, simultaneously causing bad breath, diarrhoea and general flatulence. One or two small charcoal biscuits often correct this problem.

However, none of these should take the place of cleaning the teeth with either a paste of bicarbonate of soda and salt or a canine toothpaste. Strictly speaking, canine toothbrushes are unnecessary. A small piece of material wrapped around the index finger does equally well and has the added bonus of being disposable.

There are new products on the market, alternatives to toothpaste, but as yet I have not used them. One of these products comes in a gel form and is designed to enhance the natural protective chemistry contained in saliva. The manufacturers recommend that a small, daily amount be placed in the mouth. There is no brushing or cleaning, so it sounds a great idea for dogs who dislike having their teeth cleaned. Well worth asking your vet about!

Two Dachshund anecdotes

A tooth for a tooth
Betty Cole-Hamilton

Sparky was a black-and-tan Miniature Long-haired dog who lived many years ago with his family in a boys' public school. He was a well-behaved little dog on the whole, always ready to do his share of seeing off his humans' friends: the postman, the fish man, the gardener and the like.

We did not know of his addiction to teeth until, during a large tea party at home after a school match, we became aware of a strange crunching noise coming from under a small, frilly-skirted chair. Conversation ceased as, before an interested assembled company, we discovered Sparky busily demolishing a small dental plate belonging to one of our visitors. The embarrassed but amused owner explained that, when it had begun to hurt during the match, he had surreptitiously removed it to a hankie in his pocket, only for it to fly out when a sneeze threatened at tea. To Sparky this was manna from heaven, and he could not understand the ensuing mayhem and mirth as we reclaimed his treasure.

Shortly after this a friend and I were returning by car from one of our show-raids South of the Border, and somewhere along the old A6 we stopped at a cafe for a much-needed cup of tea. We took the dogs in with us on leads, as was the custom in those good old unhygienic days. We had given our order and were waiting longingly for it to arrive when the male half of a middle-aged couple sitting nearby gave an almighty sneeze, and his entire dentistry came sliding across the floor towards us. Sparky shot out from under my chair, determined not to be thwarted a second time. For a frozen moment we sat there aghast, awaiting the canine *coup de grace*, while the teeth lay grinning fiendishly at us.

It was a close-run thing, which reduced us to such unseemly hysterics (not shared by the owner of the teeth) that there was no alternative but to make a rapid, undignified (and tea-less) exit.

Spooky but true
Betty Cole-Hamilton

We are all aware of the sensory powers our dogs possess – how emotions travel down the lead when showing, including anger and frustration, joy and pleasure. We also know the comfort we receive when our canine friends sense we are sad, grieving or ill. Psychic research is now considering whether dogs have greater power of insight than humans; I believe that this could well be the case.

A middle-aged and very practical friend of ours lived in Ludlow and owned one of our dogs, Jasper. Sometimes she walked him in the grounds of Ludlow Castle, parts of which are reputed to be haunted.

One particular day, Jasper, normally an obedient little dog, was not at her heels as expected. Looking back she saw him standing stock-still, following with his eyes the line of the Castle wall, along which the ghost or spectre of the *Lady in Grey* was said to walk. Nothing either then or subsequently would persuade Jasper to pass that place again. ESP?

4 Clubs and societies

Ch Pipersvale Chocolate Royale and Ch Jarad Chocolate Surprise at Pipersvale, owned by Betty Munt.

Owning a Dachshund is like marrying into a very large family, and walking a Dachshund is an open invitation to friendship. More than with any other breed, complete strangers will stop you in the street to look at the dog, ask questions and admire.

Within this wide-flung family are clubs devoted to the breed. Some are for Dachshunds of both sizes and all coats, and some for particular varieties. In all there are 19 different clubs for Dachshunds throughout the United Kingdom and many of them have been established for a very long time. They serve every corner of the United Kingdom, including Scotland and the Isles, Wales and Ireland.

However, no information would be complete without mentioning the most famous and respected canine club in the world: The Kennel Club.

The Kennel Club

Historical background

The middle of the 19th century found the prosperous and leisured Victorians with a passion for exhibiting and 'instructive entertainment'. The development of the railways brought The Great Exhibition of 1851, housed in what was to become Crystal Palace, within the reach of the whole of the country. Many more exhibitions of widely varying character were to follow.

The first organised dog show was held in the Town Hall, Newcastle-on-Tyne on 28-29 June 1859. The show was organised by Messrs Shorthose and Pope at the suggestion of Mr R Brailsford, and there were 60 entries of Pointers and Setters. Only one class was held for each breed at these early shows and the dogs were unidentified except for their kennel names; an entry in one of the old catalogues reads: Mr Brown's Venue, price 22/-. Unfortunately the name of the winner is not given.

The founding of The Kennel Club

Two shows were recorded each year for the next 10 years. By this time (1870) it was obvious that a controlling body was necessary to legislate in canine matters. The Crystal Palace Show was first held in 1870 by the National Dog Club and, after the second show, Mr S E Shirley, MP of Ettington, called together a committee and a discussion ensued which resulted in 12 gentlemen meeting at 2 Albert Mansions, Victoria Street, London, on 4 April 1873. This meeting marked the founding of The Kennel Club

One of the earliest undertakings of the newly-formed Kennel Club was the compilation of a stud book. The editor, Mr Frank C S Pearce, was the son of The Rev Thomas Pearce, the well known Idstone of The Field. The first volume of The Kennel Club Stud Book contained the records of shows from 1859. The Kennel Gazette was first published in 1880 and has continued as a monthly publication from that date. The Kennel Club Stud Book has been published annually, the 1996 volume being the 119th.

The committee formulated a code of 10 rules relating to dog shows, all of a simple character. It was announced that societies which adopted this code of rules for their shows would be 'recognised' and the winners at their shows would be eligible for the stud book. In 1875 the committee decided to disqualify dogs that were exhibited at unrecognised shows, but this rule was not enforced for some years.

The committee introduced many rules and regulations and, after a few years, a sound system of government was developed which was adopted by many overseas kennel clubs. HRH Edward Prince of Wales was a staunch supporter of the movement to prevent the cropping of dogs' ears and, from 9 April 1898, such dogs have been ineligible for competition under Kennel Club Rules. By the end of the century about half the competitors at dog shows were women.

Increase in dog shows

In 1900 nearly 30 championship shows were held and the smaller informal shows were

Judge Joe McCauley with Reserve CC winner Matzell Marathon owned by Mr Norton
at the Scottish Kennel Club Show 1980.

becoming more popular. The policy of the committee was to keep rules and restrictions to a minimum, and shows were recognised, licensed, or sanctioned, provided that the executive of the show signed an undertaking to hold and conduct the show under and in accordance with the rules and regulations of The Kennel Club. This still holds good today, although the categories have changed slightly.

During the past 20 years, the number of dog shows held annually in this country has increased by 50%. In 1991 approximately 500 were championship shows. In the same year approximately 350 field trials and working trials were held.

Kennel Club registration

To quote The History of the Kennel Club, it soon became obvious that some system of distinctive nomenclature would have to be introduced to overcome the confusion arising out of the quantities of Spots, Bobs, Bangs, Jets, Nettles, Vics, most of them insufficiently described and none of them being well known dogs of the same name. In 1880 the Committee introduced a system of universal registration. At first this was strongly opposed, but the advantage of reserving a name for the use of one dog only was quickly seen and accepted. Registration in 1880 was nothing more than the registration of a name to avoid duplication in the stud book; the pedigree was of little importance and only came as an aid to identification at a later date.

The number of dogs registered at The Kennel Club has increased tremendously over the years, indicating an ever-growing interest in the ownership and exhibition of pure-bred dogs. At the same time there has been a tremendous growth in the pet ownership of pure bred dogs. In recent years the average number of dogs registered with The Kennel Club has been about 250,000 a year.

The registration system has been altered during the past few years and it has been shown that the requirement is for a simple system easily understood by all. In 1981 a computer was installed to process registrations and the system has been developed to handle other Kennel Club services. The data base now comprises over 4,000,000 dog names.

The aims of The Kennel Club

The prime object of The Kennel Club is the general improvement of dogs. Its areas of authority include the classification of breeds, the registration of pedigree dogs and transfer of ownership, the licensing of shows, the framing and enforcing of Kennel Club Rules, the awarding of championship and other certificates, the registration of associations, clubs and societies seeking affiliation, and the publication of The Kennel Club Stud Book, The Kennel Club Year Book (annually) and The Kennel Gazette (monthly). While in the past the main interests have been pedigree dogs, shows and trials, recently the Club has become more concerned with 'anti-dog' legislation and it actively represents the interests of responsible dog owners whether or not the dog is Kennel Club registered. The Canine Code was published some few years ago and The Kennel Club Good Citizen Dog Scheme is a further milestone in The Kennel Club's policy of education toward responsible ownership.

The Kennel Club has its finger on the pulse of the canine world and serves its community devotedly. Like all governing bodies, it has its detractors. However, perhaps we should consider that it is impossible to please all the people all the time.

Kennel Club regulations concerning such areas as registration of puppies, transfer of ownership, and the necessary paperwork involved are necessarily complicated and too detailed to be included here. However, you can rest assured that a telephone call to The Kennel Club on any subject concerning your dog, its welfare, registration or pedigree will receive immediate attention from the dedicated staff at the other end of the line. (See Useful Addresses)

Dachshund breed clubs

The oldest established club in our breed is The Dachshund Club itself, with membership throughout Britain. It is possible to belong to more than one club, and many members who belong to their own regional club are also members of The Dachshund Club.

There are many advantages to belonging to a club. One is that you will be kept up-to-date on all the news. Another is that you will be sent schedules for all the shows these clubs sponsor. Yet another is that clubs are places where you can seek knowledgeable advice on all subjects relating to your own breed of Dachshund, including showing, show venues and even Kennel Club rules and regulations. Kennel Club rules can be a minefield to the novice. It is good to have someone in the breed who, for the price of a telephone call, will keep you on the straight and narrow.

Breed clubs hold social occasions and teach-ins. They also hold small match shows, in which other clubs are invited to show alongside you, and these are ideal for gaining confidence. Such occasions are great fun and often, over tea and a bun, you are given the opportunity to ask questions. With teach-ins you have the benefit of experienced handlers and judges who are always generous with their advice. They may advise you how to handle your dog to best advantage. No Dachshund is perfect, but perfection is something for which we all strive. With Long-haired and Wire-haired Dachshunds there is a great deal to learn about presentation. Preparation of the coat before showing is an art form and can make the world of difference.

Many of these clubs produce newsletters, club publications, cassettes and publicity items such as car windscreen stickers and badges. All are sold at a reasonable price, which helps top up Club funds.

The Dachshund Club

This club has an interesting history. It was founded on 17 January 1881, when Mr Arkwright, Major Harry Jones, The Rev G F Lovell and Mr Montague Wooten met at Cox's Hotel, Jermyn Street, London. Mr Montague Wooten was elected as the first Hon Secretary. This makes The Dachshund Club the oldest Dachshund breed club in the world.

The club publishes in hardcover The Dachshund Club Handbook and Records, which few in any breed can equal in volume or scope for information. It provides a permanent record of the achievements of current breeders and exhibitors. The club also promotes two prestigious shows, a championship and open show, each year. The Dachshund Club also has the very great honour of having HRH Queen Elizabeth the Queen Mother as one of its Honorary Members.

The affairs of the club are conducted by an executive committee elected by postal ballet of the whole club prior to the annual general meeting, held in London in the Spring of each year. Half the committee members retire annually but are eligible for re-election. The AGM is usually preceded by a club luncheon.

The Club seeks to encourage the breeding of the correct type of Dachshund for sport and show, and to ensure competent judges to officiate at shows.

The Northern Dachshund Association

This is the second oldest Dachshund breed club in Great Britain, registered with The Kennel Club in 1899.

The Scottish Dachshund Club

The Scottish Dachshund Club was founded in 1902. This club serves a widely scattered membership, including the Scottish Isles.

Each year the Scottish Dachshund Club offers its members two shows: a championship show in Dumfries in the spring, and an open show in Edinburgh in the autumn. It represents all six varieties of Dachshunds. A members' luncheon precedes their

Jill Johnstone (Silvae) looking at her CC wnners
at the Northern Dachshund Association Show 1981.

AGM each year, offering an excellent opportunity for everyone to meet, away from the pressures of the ring.

In the early days, Veronica Collins, who was a well-known Dachshund enthusiast, worked very hard as Convenor to bring about the popularity the club now enjoys. She was aided by such notables as Miss Muriel Stewart (Vice Convener) and Miss Jean Cook of the famous Deugh affix (Hon Secretary). To date, however, no one has worked harder than Mrs Jean McNaughton of the Cedavoch affix. In 1963 she, as Hon Secretary, and her husband Don as Treasurer, worked in close collaboration to further the breed. His death was a hard blow to the Club, but Jean demonstrated great courage at this time by continuing his work.

The Scottish Dachshund Club offers teach-ins and advice on all matters pertaining to Dachshunds, including a puppy sales service to all members and those people looking for puppies.

The Dachshund Club of Wales

This is a relative newcomer, founded in 1972. A pace-setting and friendly club, The Dachshund Club of Wales caters for all six varieties of Dachshunds throughout the United Kingdom, many members beyond the boundaries of Wales. It circulates a highly readable Newsletter to all its members and provides distinctive badges and car-stickers. Most informative and useful is the Club's illustrated calender, which includes a show-goer's diary of events. They also run a caring rescue service.

The Ulster Dachshund Club

This Club was founded in 1946 and extends a truly Irish welcome to all who join. Catering for all six varieties of Dachshunds, the Club encourages all newcomers and hold monthly Matches with all other clubs.They also hold an annual open show with Cups and Specials on offer.

Others

The clubs already mentioned cover every area in the United Kingdom, but that does not mean that other clubs are less important. Dachshund breed clubs can be found throughout the United Kingdom and every area is represented. They have much to offer the new owner of a Dachshund, whether potential exhibitor or pet owner. As we have already said, owning a Dachshund is akin to belonging to a very large family.

Useful names, addresses and telephone numbers for the nearest Club in your area are all available from The Kennel Club, London (see Useful Addresses).

Rescue

The Dachshund Rescue Service
Valerie Skinner (Ritterburg)

Dachshund Rescue is run in alliance with The Dachshund Club and The Long-haired Dachshund Club. It is first mentioned in the minutes of a committee meeting held by The Dachshund Club in January 1968. Miss Walsh proposed that the club start a rescue service. The meeting was in full sympathy with the proposal, and several members immediately offered their help. Later, in September 1971, the question was again raised by Mrs B Beaumont, and the Secretary was asked to approach The Long-haired Dachshund Club with a view to the venture, so the Dachshund Rescue Service became official. It represents a combined effort between the two clubs with a joint committee. Founder committee members Mrs M Rhodes, Miss K Raine (known as Molly to her friends and author of All About Dachshunds) and Mrs B Beaumont proceeded to open a bank account in the name of Rescue Service, to which equal contributions were made by both Clubs. In 1973, Mrs Rhodes took on the rôle of Secretary and Treasurer. By that time as many as 20 Dachshunds were successfully re-settled into new homes.

In the early days, Dachshunds were usually re-homed by word of mouth, person to person, and a careful list was kept of all Dachshunds in need of re-homing. These people were then put in touch with owners willing to take on one of these animals. If the need arose, the dogs were boarded out until a suitable home could be found.

Katherine 'Molly' Raine was deeply involved in this work for many years but, in 1986, it was decided that the work load would have to be divided between north and south. The number of Dachshunds had risen with each year to 125, and Mr T Webster took up the position as an independent Treasurer.

I took over the rescue service for the north in 1987, and Diane Moate took over the south. Mrs Moate was later followed by Elizabeth Heeson, who was then succeeded by Stella Clarke.

By the year 1991, the rescue figures peaked to 153, although, thankfully there is now a definite downward trend; by 1995 they had dropped again to 104. The figures do not necessarily reflect an escalation of neglect or cruelty. If you take into account the rising popularity of the breed (in 1994–1995, 9829 Dachshund of all varieties were registered with The Kennel Club in London) and the life expectancy of a Dachshund (10–15 years) you get some idea of how many Dachshunds there are in the United Kingdom. Dachshunds are rehomed for many reasons and, thankfully, very few come to us through cruelty, domestic mishandling or straying. A good number are because of the death or sickness of elderly owners; that is, cases where the deceased's family cannot cope. Neither does the service entirely consist of re-settling. The Dachshund Helpline is kept busy with all kind of enquiries dealing with every aspect of dog owning, training and behavioural problems. Sometimes The Dachshund rescue service is simply there to lend a sympathetic ear when someone is in floods of tears over the death of a much-loved pet. In many cases a beloved Dachshund is the only friend and companion that person had.

Overall, the rescue service runs very smoothly. Dachshunds can be taken into care straight away and given all the veterinary attention they need. Happily, in the case of healthy Dachshunds, they are usually rehomed in a matter of days, although we have to say that some of our more elderly citizens take a little longer. In all cases, we are careful to place the right dog with the right owners.

Thankfully, we are financially sound, and this is due to our many fund raisers and supporters, our transport helpers, and all those people who have the welfare of the breed at heart. I am sure that those involved in founding the service some 28 years ago would take great comfort in the knowledge that their brainchild is so successful today.

The National Canine Defence League

Most people will have heard the slogan coined by The National Canine Defence League, *A dog is for life*. Dogs should never be given as gifts, particularly unasked and unwanted gifts. You may find that buying a Dachshund around Christmas time is difficult. This is no coincidence: few responsible Dachshund breeders want their dogs going to homes not

Ch Pipersvale A Trifle Tipsy.

prepared for them. In my opinion, a puppy should never be a surprise gift except under extenuating circumstances. It is better by far to arrange with the breeder to present the pedigree rather than the puppy to the recipient, and then both giver and recipient have the opportunity of collecting the dog.

Novice breeders are urged always to take every precaution when selling a puppy. Do not be afraid to ask searching questions and to seek proof of track record from a would-be buyer. Never sell to a stranger who cannot provide an adequate reference, be it from someone else in the breed or a vet. Do be careful: people who have come forward with

Ch Razzle Dazzle at Pipersvale.

the most plausible stories have been known to sell the unfortunate puppy on to someone whose reputation should bar him or her forever from owning a dog. The puppy is then sold on to third or even fourth parties, and the profits can be considerable. Fortunately, with Dachshunds there is usually a grape-vine where such people are at work, so breeders can be fore-warned.

Among its many charitable activities on behalf of dogs, The National Canine Defence League works hard to eradicate the practice of puppy farming. Its leaflet *Condemned to Death* makes harrowing reading. To quote:

In the UK today, thousands of puppies are bred in appalling 'battery farm' conditions – often from unhealthy mothers who are used as 'puppy producing machines'.

Puppy farms profit from intensive and indiscriminate mass breeding. Estimates suggest there are thousands of puppy farms in the UK – some with as many as 150 breeding bitches.

The pups are either sold through newspaper advertisements or transported to pet shops and 'superstores', where they are sold at high prices to unsuspecting dog lovers.

This practice can only survive if these people are encouraged by prospective owners who buy from them. The answer must be to buy from a breeder who has been highly recommended by someone you know and trust. Insist on seeing the mother of the pups, be aware of the set up as a whole, the health of the other animals on the premises – and, however sorry you might feel for a particular puppy, don't buy it out of sympathy. By 'rescuing' such a pup you will be encouraging the practice and courting disaster. Many people have purchased such animals, only to have them fall ill of inheritable disorders and latent diseases such as mental trauma, blindness and congenital heart diseases.

If you have a charity in mind, do consider the work of the NCDL, which exists to protect and defend all dogs from abuse, cruelty, abandonment and any form of mistreatment, in Great Britain and abroad. It also produces informative leaflets on such subjects as *What makes a good breeder?*

Do make yourself aware; be vigilant. Better still, help the NCDL wipe out puppy farms by making a donation or by becoming a campaigner. For further details and information about The National Canine Defence League, contact Selena Makepeace at the NCDL Press Office. (See Useful Addresses.)

An armful of Maricturs.

5 Recognised Breed Standards

The Kennel Club Breed Standard – Dachshunds

Copies of the Breed standards for all dogs are available from The Kennel Club. You can also pick up a copy of *Breed Standards (Hound Group)* at most Championship Shows for a very small cost. The Kennel Club stall offers all kinds of information and is well worth a visit.

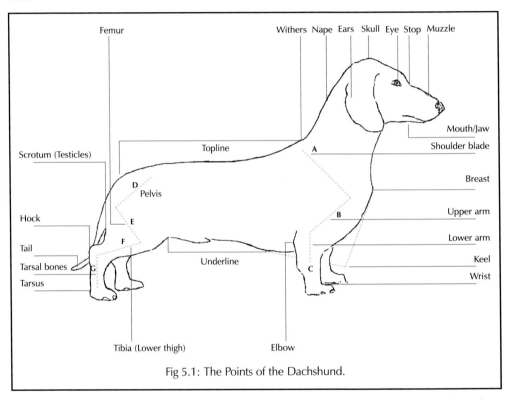

Fig 5.1: The Points of the Dachshund.

The Kennel Club is the parent, if you like, for all breeds. As such it sets the rules, standards and regulations. For immediate reference and with the very kind permission of The Kennel Club, the standard is set out in full below. The line drawing in Fig 5.1 shows the points of the Dachshund and Figs 5.2 and 5.3 show its skeleton and musculature:

General Appearance: Long and low, but with compact, well muscled body, bold, defiant carriage of head and intelligent expression.

Characteristics: Intelligent, lively, courageous to the point of rashness, obedient. Especially suited to going to ground because of low build, very strong forequarters and forelegs. Long, strong jaw, and immense power of bite and hold. Excellent nose, persevering hunter and tracker.

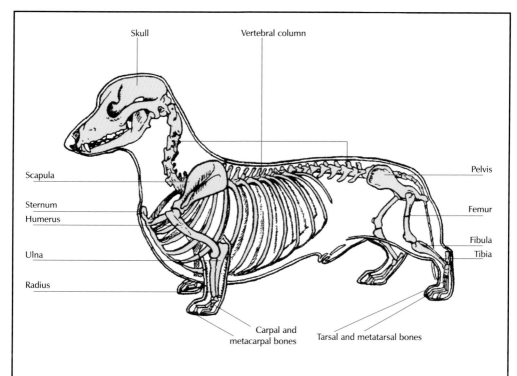

Fig 5.2 (above): Skeleton of the Dachshund.

Fig 5.3 (below): Musculature of the Dachshund.

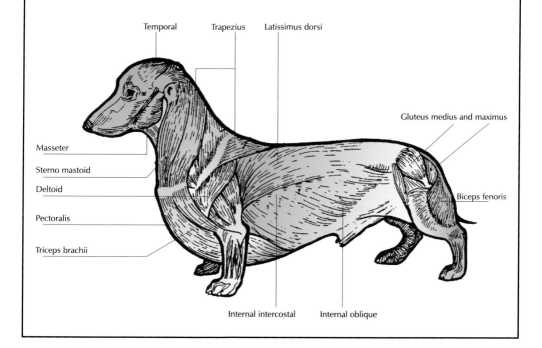

Standard Smooth: Ch Marictur Marriott.

Temperament: Faithful, versatile and good tempered.

Head and skull: Long, appearing conical when seen from above; from side tapering uniformly to tip of nose. Skull only slightly arched. Neither too broad nor too narrow, sloping gradually without prominent stop into slightly arched muzzle. Length from tip of nose to eyes equal to length from eyes to occiput. In Wire haired, particularly, ridges over eyes strongly prominent, giving appearance of slightly broader skull. Lips well stretched, neatly covering lower jaw. Strong jaw bones not too square or snipey, but open wide.

Eyes: Medium size, almond shaped, set obliquely. Dark except in chocolates, where they can be lighter. In Dapples one or both 'wall' eyes permissible.

Ears: Set high, and not too far forward. Broad, of moderate length, and well rounded (not pointed or folded). Forward edge touching cheek. Mobile, and when at attention back of ear directed forward and outward.

Mouth: Teeth strongly developed, powerful canine teeth fitting closely. Jaws strong, with perfect, regular and complete scissor bite, ie upper teeth closely overlapping lower teeth and set square to the jaws. Complete dentition important.

Neck: Long, muscular, clean with no dewlap, slightly arched, running in graceful lines into shoulders, carried proudly forward.

Forequarters: Shoulder blades long, broad, and placed firmly and obliquely (45 degrees to the horizontal) upon very robust rib cage. Upper arm the same length as shoulder blade, set at 90 degrees to it, very strong, and covered with hard, supple muscles. Upper arm lies close to ribs, but able to move freely. Forearm short and strong in bone, inclining slightly inwards; when seen in profile moderately straight, must not bend forward or knuckle over, which indicates unsoundness. Correctly placed foreleg should cover the lowest point of the keel.

Body: Long and full muscled. Back level, with slightly sloping shoulders, lying in straightest possible line between withers and sightly arched loin. Loin short and strong. Breast bone strong, and so prominent that a depression appears on either side of it in front. When viewed from front, thorax full and oval; when viewed from side or above, full volumed, so allowing by its ample capacity complete development of heart and lungs.Well ribbed up, underline gradually merging into line of abdomen. Body sufficiently clear of the ground to allow free movement.

Hindquarters: Rump full, broad and strong, pliant muscles. Croup long, full, robustly muscled, only slightly sloping towards tail. Pelvis strong, set obliquely and not too short. Upper thigh set at right angles to pelvis, strong and of good length. Lower thigh short, set at right angles to upper thigh and well muscled. Legs when seen behind set well apart, straight, and parallel. Hind dewclaws undesirable.

Feet: Front feet full, broad, deep, close knit, straight or very slightly turned out. Hindfeet small and narrower. Toes close together, with a decided arch to each toe, strong regularly placed nails, thick and firm pads. Dogs must stand true, ie equally on all parts of the foot.

Tail: Continues line of spine, but slightly curved, without kinks or twists, not carried too high, or touching ground when at rest.

Miniature Wire: Ch Bothlyn Blue Grass.

Gait/Movement: Should be free and flowing. Stride should be long, with the drive coming from behind the hindquarters when viewed from the side. Viewed from in front or behind, the legs and feet should move parallel to each other with the distance apart being the width of the shoulder and hip joints respectively.

Coat:

Smooth-Haired: Dense, short and smooth. Hair on underside of tail coarse in texture. Skin loose and supple, but fitting closely all over without dewlap and little or no wrinkle.

Long-Haired: Soft and straight, or only slightly waved; longest under neck, on underparts of body, and behind legs, where it forms abundant feathering, on tail where it forms a flag. Outside of ears well feathered. Coat flat, and not obscuring outline. Too much hair on feet undesirable.

Wire-Haired: With exception of jaw, eyebrows, chin and ears, the whole body should be covered with a short, straight, harsh coat with dense undercoat, beard on chin, eyebrows bushy, but hair on ears almost smooth. Legs and feet well but neatly furnished with harsh coat.

Colour: All colours allowed but (except in dapples which should be evenly marked all over) no white permissible, save for a small patch on chest which is permissible but not desirable. Nose and nails black in all colours except chocolate/tan and chocolate/dapple, where brown permitted.

Size:

Standards: Ideal weight: 9-12kg (20-26lb)

Miniatures Ideal weight: 4.5kg (10lb) It is of the utmost importance that judges should not award prizes to animals over 5kg.

Faults: Any departure from the foregoing points should be considered a fault and the seriousness with which the fault should be regarded should be in exact proportion to its degree.

Note: Male animals should have two apparently normal testicles fully descended into the scrotum.

The Illustrated Standard of Points of the Dachshund of All Varieties
Explanatory notes by John Feetham Sayer and diagrams by J P Sayer
Reproduced by permission of The Dachshund Club

I think it is true to say that The Illustrated Standard of Points of the Dachshund Of All Varieties has become over the years the Dachshund 'Bible'. While this book is entitled The Contemporary Dachshund and deals with present-day developments, the substance of Sayer's work is still relevant. It should be noted that The Kennel Club Breed Standard was revised in 1987, and differs in some details from that quoted by Mr Sayer. However, it remains similar in the basic principle, as was stressed by Rosalind A Rawson in her notes on Sayer's sixth edition in 1994. We therefore offer an abridged version of his work which, while condensed, is still true to the original – Compiler.

General appearance

Rule: Long and low, but with compact and well-muscled body, neither crippled, cloddy, nor clumsy, with bold, defiant carriage of head and intelligent expression.

Note: This description always strikes me as somewhat inadequate to express the general appearance of the breed, to differentiate it from other breeds of earth-dogs – that is, dogs that are primarily used for hunting their prey in burrows underground. For instance, it omits a reference to its heavy bone, its large feet and the pendulous ears that bespeak its hound origin and account for its adaptability to field hunting and tracking. Here a good nose and persevering nature render it particularly useful, in addition to its ability to work underground, at which it is expert. The distinctive feature of lowness refers to its height at the shoulder, or general line of back, and must not be confused with the depth of the chest which, if exaggerated, may be too near the ground and so impede the free action of the legs.

The intelligent expression bespoken by the bold, defiant carriage of head should be cultivated as far as possible by showing the dog 'sport' in some form, even if only small vermin.

Head and skull

Rule: Long, and appearing conical when seen from above, and from the side view tapering to the point of the muzzle. Stop not pronounced and the skull should be slightly arched in profile, and appearing neither too broad nor too narrow.

Note: There are many forms of heads, good and bad, too numerous to illustrate, so I content myself by showing the ideal in fig 5.4a and two incorrect examples: in fig 5.4b, showing too much stop, and fig 5.4c, showing short, snipy jaw and high set ears. Fig 5.4d (dewlap) is referred to in the notes for the neck.

The *stop* referred to is that part of the head between the eyebrows where the upper jaw joins the skull. Here there should be a decided drop in the line between skull and jaw, and the less the stop the better and more typical the head (refer to fig 5.4b). The bridge-bones over the eyes (eyebrows) should be strongly prominent, but must not be confused with the stop.

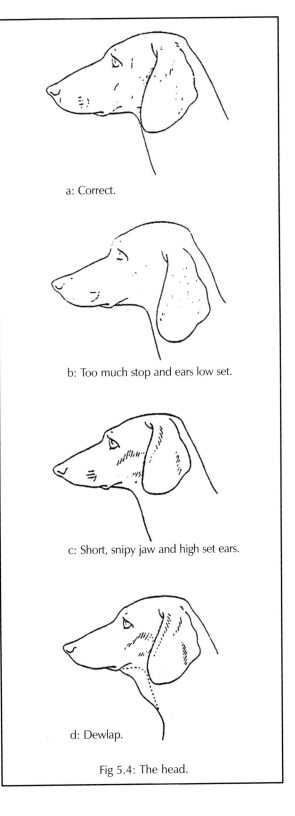

a: Correct.

b: Too much stop and ears low set.

c: Short, snipy jaw and high set ears.

d: Dewlap.

Fig 5.4: The head.

In a well-proportioned head the skull and the jaw will be of approximately equal length; in other words, from the back of the skull to the eyes should be the same length as from the eyes to the end of the nose (see fig 5.4a). The question of jaw is referred to below.

Jaw

Rule: Neither too square nor snipy, but strong, lips lightly stretched, fairly covering the lower jaw.

Notes: This is a very short, even meagre, rule but, taken in conjunction with that for the skull, it will be found sufficiently informative. The strength of the jaw depends on the strength of the muscles along the sides of the skull; length adds to strength in a muscle and a long skull ensures length of muscle and consequent strength to the jaw if of correct form. The jaw should be capable of being widely opened, and the fulcrum (the point at which the upper and lower jaws hinge), being on a vertical line behind the eyes, allows for this. Seen from above, the jaw should taper uniformly to the nose (fig 5.5a) and not be pinched between the eye and nose (fig 5.5b). The ridge of the upper jaw should be long and narrow. From a side view the muzzle should have a slight arch; a perfectly straight muzzle is not desirable.

The form of the jaw is to a considerable extent dependent on the dentition, but strangely enough no rule was given for dentition in the original standard. This omission has been rectified and a new rule added under the title Dentition.

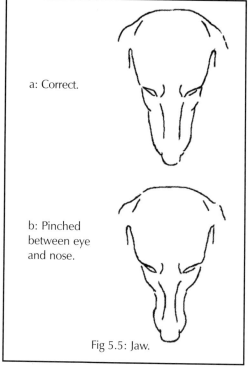

a: Correct.

b: Pinched between eye and nose.

Fig 5.5: Jaw.

Dentition

Rule: Teeth must be strongly developed; the powerful canine teeth must fit exactly into one another; the back or inner side of the upper front teeth must rest closely on the front side of the under teeth.

Notes: The correct fitting of the front teeth has been described as the scissor bite, any deviation from this being a fault. Strong, correctly placed teeth are of the utmost importance to a dog that has to meet fox or badger in mortal combat in the burrow. Particular attention should be given to the structure of the mouths of the exhibits. A cursory glance, or feel with the fingers is not enough. The whole form and set of the teeth should be carefully examined, and any deviation from the rule should be noted and reported on for the benefit of the breeders. Unhappily some judges, British and foreign,

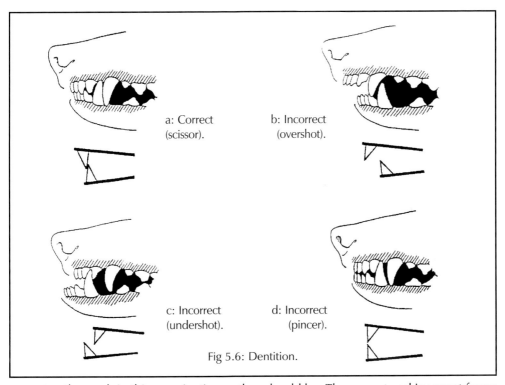

a: Correct (scissor).

b: Incorrect (overshot).

c: Incorrect (undershot).

d: Incorrect (pincer).

Fig 5.6: Dentition.

are not as thorough in this examination as they should be. The correct and incorrect forms are illustrated in fig 5.6. In the correct form (fig 5.6a) the canine teeth fit together exactly, the upper teeth resting closely in front of the lower set. This ensures an immensely powerful grip. Fig 5.6b shows an overshot jaw, purposely drawn in a somewhat exaggerated form so that no reader can be in any doubt about what an overshot jaw is, but at the same time it must be borne in mind that, if the upper and lower teeth don't fit quite closely, the jaw is slightly overshot. Fig 5.6c shows an undershot jaw, a comparatively rare form. A bad case would give too square a finish to the end of the jaw, which is both incorrect and ugly. Fig 5.6d shows pincer teeth, so called because the upper and lower front teeth meet exactly edge to edge. This form is comparatively rare, but definitely faulty. Distemper teeth, more or less decayed, are also faulty, though to a lesser degree.

I am aware that some breeders in this country and on the Continent disagree with the thesis that pincer teeth are faulty but, as the German standard which we adopt in essence was framed by experts who used the dog for sport, we must accept their ruling and judge by it. I am not prepared to say that I would debar a dog with pincer teeth from the prize list but I would hesitate to place it high in the awards.

Eyes
Rule: Medium in size, oval, and set obliquely. Dark in colour, except in the case of chocolates, where they may be lighter, and in dapples, where one or both wall eyes are permissible.

Notes: Light eyes are said to spoil the expression but, without wholly disagreeing with this opinion shared by many judges, I would point out that, if the eyes are deeply set under the eyebrow as they should be, and are not large, staring, or goggle-eyed, they can have little effect on the expression. Light eyes are not so spoiling to the expression as a flesh-coloured nose would be.

Ears
Rule: Broad, of moderate length and well rounded (not narrow, pointed or folded), relatively well back, high, and well set on, lying close to the cheek, very mobile as in all intelligent dogs, when at attention the back of the ear directed forwards and outwards.
Notes: This rule is sufficiently explicit and I need only draw attention to fig 5.4b. This shows a low set on the ear, which is also folded (does not rest flat against the cheek). Such ears are often too long and floppy and give a soft expression to the head. On the other hand, a short, high-set ear gives a terrier expression (fig 5.4c) and is equally wrong. Ears that stand out from the cheeks are also faulty.

Neck
Rule: Sufficiently long, muscular, clean, no dewlap, slightly arched in the nape, running in graceful lines into the shoulders, carried well up and forward.
Notes: Fig 5.4d displays dewlap, or bagginess of the skin of the neck. Where this occurs it is usually (but not always) accompanied by some wrinkles on the forelegs and sometimes on the skull. The skin should fit closely to the body all over but be elastic when handled.

A thin or ewe neck, with no arch in the nape, is quite wrong and very ugly, as is a short thick one, which is often associated with a short back. A short thick neck gives a stuffy appearance to the whole figure.

Forequarters
Rule: Shoulder-blades long, broad, and set on sloping, lying firmly on full-developed ribs or thorax, muscles hard and plastic. Chest very oval, with ample room for heart and lungs, deep and well sprung out ribs toward the loins, breastbone very prominent, and the front legs should, when viewed from one side, cover the lowest part of the breast line.
Notes: The forequarters are of very great importance in the anatomical structure of the body to ensure strength and endurance for work underground, and the diagrams should be carefully studied in conjunction with this rule (figs 5.7 and 5.8).

The word supple, meaning pliant and flexible, is perhaps better than plastic to express the actions of the muscles.

All through the standard it is laid down that the dog should be muscular and, especially in the fore- and hindquarters, the muscle should stand out clearly to the eye and not be overlaid by fat. A lean dog shows its muscles if they are well developed and in hard condition. Muscular development depends on continuous exercise and exertion.

To give the necessary heart and lung room, the thorax, or chest as is commonly called, must be capacious and the ribs full volumed. The front must be broad, deep and long. The point of the breastbone should be high up, prominent and carried in a graceful curve down through the forelegs and well back toward the abdomen. At its lowest part between the forelegs it should not be lower than the wrist, commonly called the knee, and only in a fully developed dog should it extend that far. Breeders who seek to hurry on the development of their young bitches by early breeding are surely misguided. It is much more desirable that young growing dogs are left to develop naturally and gradually, and so build up and maintain their strength. If the forequarters are correctly formed to start with, development will come with age. It is not necessary for the chest to be as low as the wrist; the whole requirement is that it should be full volumed (very oval).

In fig 5.7a is shown the ideal formation of the forequarters in profile, and from the front in fig 5.7c. In fig 5.7b a diagram of the skeleton illustrates the correct shape and length of the breastbone.

It is wrong if the chest is too narrow, as in fig 5.8c, or too broad, though the former is the worst fault, giving what the Germans call a *chicken-breast* and constricting the thorax.

In connection with the depth of the chest, one often reads in the reports of critics at the shows that a dog is *very low to ground*. This is intended as a compliment, but I fear it usually means that the dog has a very deep chest, a fault rather than a virtue. One of the dangers at shows where competition is very keen is that, in points where much is required, more is thought to be better, so exaggeration creeps in and is boomed where it ought to be damned. There are nine true ribs and four false ones on each side but, in a short breastbone, there is a deficiency of rib and a consequent constriction of capacity in the thorax, a bad fault.

The prominence of the breastbone in front gives a long, sloping shoulder, whereas a flat front where the breastbone is not prominent gives a short, upright shoulder and consequently a wrong angulation of the forelegs, referred to under the rule for the legs, which follows later. Fig 5.7a has a dotted line under it to show the extent from front to back, towards the abdomen, of the breastbone.

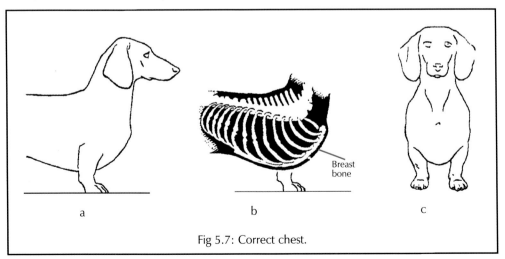

Breast bone

a   b   c

Fig 5.7: Correct chest.

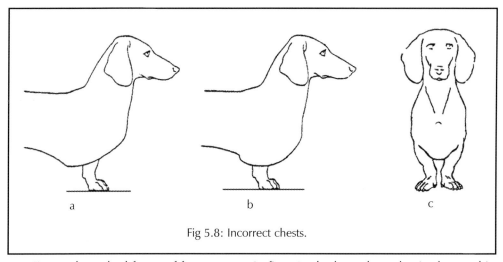

a   b   c

Fig 5.8: Incorrect chests.

Fig 5.8 shows bad forms of forequarters. In fig 5.8a the breastbone begins low and is not prominent; it is short and comes down to a point behind the legs. The example in fig 5.8b is especially bad. Both examples show restricted thoraxes and are to be condemned severely. There are other gradations of inferiority in this region, but those illustrated are perhaps the worst. Any variations from the ideal fig 5.7a should be penalised. Seen from the front the chest should be very oval and comparatively broad, the legs closely associated with the ribs down to the wrists, or knees as they are styled, and thence straight and well apart to afford a sturdy stance (fig 5.7c).

Fig 5.8c depicts a narrow front with forelegs too close together at the wrist and the feet splayed outwards to give stability. This is a weak formation. Fig 5.9d (see Legs and Feet) shows the elbows standing out from the ribs.

To gauge more correctly the shape and length of the breastbone, which governs the depth of chest it is best, when judging to sit or squat in the ring to bring the eye as low as is conveniently possible to the general line of the back of the dog. In this position one obtains a truer view of its build than is possible in a standing position. This is not a question of the physical proportions of the judge. It is common sense, and is done by several judges, both Continental and British, in this and other breeds of short-legged dogs.

Legs and feet

Rule: Forelegs very short and, in proportion to size, strong in bone. Upper arm of equal length with, and at right angles to the shoulder blade, elbows lying close to ribs but moving freely up to shoulder blades. Lower arm short as compared with other animals, slightly inclined inwards (crook), seen in profile moderately straight, not bending forward or knuckling over (unsoundness), feet large, round and strong with thick pads, toes compact and with distinct arch in each toe, nails strong, smaller and narrower hind feet. The dog must stand true, ie equally on all parts of the foot.

Note: This rule refers principally to the forelegs and feet. It is very full and explicit. It begins with forelegs very short... but here again exaggeration is dangerous. Shortness of leg is not

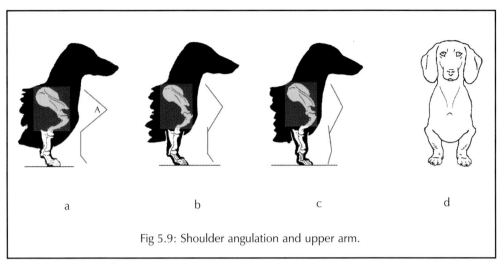

a   b   c   d

Fig 5.9: Shoulder angulation and upper arm.

in itself a merit; beyond a certain extent it is a handicap. What is required in an earth dog is a low centre of gravity to enable it to work under low, overhanging ledges and in cramped quarters. This is obtained by the bones in the upper arm and shoulder being joined at right angles, giving the greatest possible length of leg without losing the low gravity.

The correct angulation of the shoulders and upper arm is illustrated in fig 5.9a, together with the wrong form in fig 5.9b, where the shoulder is too steep and the upper arm is joined to it in an obtuse angle, rendering the forequarters less firm. This may lead to knuckling over of the forelegs and, in bad cases (Fig 5.9c), may cause the elbows to stand out from the ribs (fig 5.9d) because of bad angulation, throwing undue weight onto the lower leg. The body should rest over the legs and not hang loosely between them.

A right-angled formation of the shoulder and upper arm ensures a firmer stance than an obtuse angle would do and the elbows are less likely to stand out from weakness or any other cause.

The correct angulation is easy to gauge by the width between the point of the breastbone in front to the back of the shoulder at the top, as shown in fig 5.9a, which illustrates the correct form. Compare it with fig 5.9b, where the shoulder is too steep, the point of the breastbone is not prominent, and the are legs too far forward.

The pasterns project the feet somewhat forward, and in that the Dachshund differs from the Terrier. It is very important that the forefeet are correctly formed: large, round and close-knit, with firm pads underneath, giving a distinct arch to each toe (fig 5.10 – overleaf). There are five toes, but only four are in use. A small, round, terrier foot is not correct, nor is a long, narrow one (fig 5.11 – overleaf), sometimes called a hare foot. In the former it is easier to get soundness; in the latter the feet are more prone to become flat and spread or twisted outwards.

The feet may be slightly turned outwards or quite straight, but never turned inwards, as may sometimes be seen in moving. In a bad case this is aptly described as *plaiting* – throwing one foot over the other.

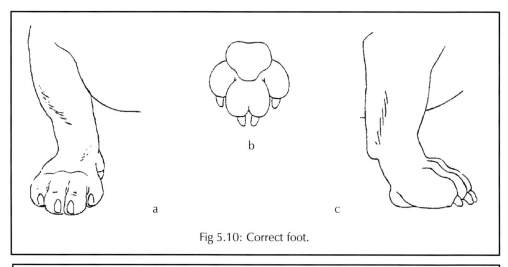

Fig 5.10: Correct foot.

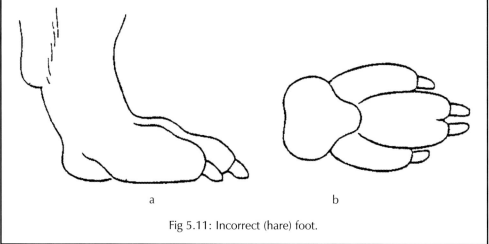

Fig 5.11: Incorrect (hare) foot.

The desired arching on the toes depends on the hardness of the pads under them, and this hardness depends on road exercise. An insufficiently exercised dog, will have soft pads, which let down the arch of the toes and, in bad cases, cause them to appear flat and open. Incorrect size and shape should be regarded as a serious fault, and I stress *size*.

The bone of the forelegs should be comparatively heavy but proportionate to the size of the dog: strong, round bone. The skin on the forelegs should fit like a glove and not be wrinkled, a prevailing fault not confined to our home-bred dogs.

Body trunk

Rule: Long and muscular, the line of the back slightly depressed at the shoulders, and slightly arched over the loin, which should be short and strong, outline of belly moderately tucked up.

Notes: Modern fashion has decreed that the line of the back should be perfectly level, and this would appear to be a contradiction of the rule, but in reality is nothing more than a loose generalisation. The whole lie of the back from the withers to the rump should never be *dead level*. The German standards puts the rule more clearly and unmistakably: *The back with sloping shoulders should lie in the straightest possible line between the withers and the slightly arched loins, these latter being short, rigid and broad.* What is required is a general levelness of the back, the hindquarters and rump, none being higher than the shoulders.

If a dog has a perfectly flat back throughout it may border on the hollow, a weak feature. It seems necessary to stress this fact because one often reads notices in which even a slight rise over the loin is regarded as a fault, and sometimes even styled a roach, thereby displaying the writer's ignorance; and to refer in praise to a back being dead level is no less a misstatement of the correct form. The under line of the body should not be excessively drawn up to the abdomen like a Greyhound.

Fig 5.12a depicts what I consider the ideal outline, from stem to stern, of the whole dog. This illustration is taken from a living dog, but somewhat idealised.

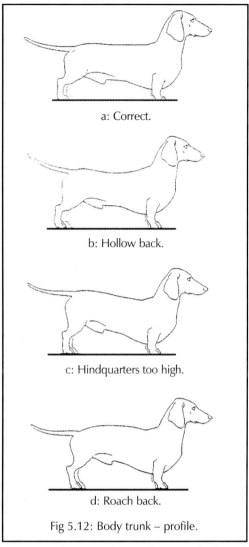

a: Correct.

b: Hollow back.

c: Hindquarters too high.

d: Roach back.

Fig 5.12: Body trunk – profile.

There are many variations from the ideal, ranging from nearly good to very bad, and in Figs 5.12b–d I show three glaringly bad faults. Fig 5.12b shows a *hollow back* – a weak form. Fig 5.12c shows *hindquarters higher than the shoulders.* These two are the most common. A dog that has only a slight tendency to a hollow back is often referred to by critics, who fear to be blunt, as being *soft in back*, but this description should deceive no one. Fig 5.12d shows a *roach back*, where the back has a continuous arch from the withers to the rump. This form is rarely seen, fortunately.

It is characteristic of the breed that the body - the middle piece - should be long and muscular. This is referred to in General appearance.

Insufficient length of body combined with short legs and a deep chest gives a cloddy appearance; and on the other hand undue length of body and too heavy bone may make for clumsiness. What is required is just enough of both to ensure a well-balanced figure.

Hindquarters

Rule: Rump round, full, broad; muscles hard and plastic; hip bone or pelvis bone not too short, broad and strongly developed, set moderately sloping; thigh-bones strong, of good length and joined to pelvis at right angles; lower thighs short in comparison with other animals; hocks well developed and seen from behind the legs should be straight (not cow-hocked); hindfeet smaller in bone and narrower than fore feet. The dog should not appear higher at quarters than at shoulder.

Notes: It is of the greatest importance that the hindquarters, whence springs the propelling power of the whole machine, are correctly angulated and compact, to afford strength and sturdiness. The rule is very clearly expressed and, if read with the diagrams before you, should be quite easily understood.

As with the forequarters, everything depends on the angulation of the bones. In fig 5.13a the pelvis is long and set moderately sloping, and the thigh bone is at a right angle to it. The shin-bone or lower leg is of such length that the hock stands just clear of the back of the thigh, with the foot bones standing perpendicularly up to the hock, and, with due width of rump as shown in Fig 5.14a, the whole gives power and compact figure.

On the other hand, fig 5.13b shows a short pelvis and the thigh-bone to it an obtuse angle and this gives a narrow figure as shown by the dotted lines. If the shin-bone is too short, as indicated in this figure, the back of the thigh overhangs the hock and the movement is cramped and awkward. However, with an obtuse angle formation the shin-bone is more usually of a normal length, causing the hock to project too far behind the back of the thigh (fig 5.13c) and the hindquarters appear to be loosely tacked onto the body. As a critic has expressed it, *the thighs seem to trail behind*. I must add that this defective form of the hindquarters, though too often seen, is not confined to dogs bred in this country.

Fig 5.13d shows the pelvic-bone set too sloping, as may be gauged by the low-set of the tail. With a long shin-bone and foot bones, the leg takes on what is called a *sicklehock*: a weak formation often seen in connection with a *cow-hock* (fig 5.14c), but not invariably. The cow-hock is the worst feature in the hindquarters, expressing weakness in a vital part.

Fig 5.14a shows the correct sturdy hindquarters with a broad rump viewed from behind, the thighs well developed and muscular and the legs well apart but straight up to the hocks. In moving, the legs should go straight ahead like the piston rods of a locomotive, and the feet should turn neither in nor out.

Fig 5.14b shows narrow hindquarters with the legs too close together and the feet outwards: a weak formation. Fig 5.14d shows bandy legs with the feet turning inwards. There are other bad forms, but I trust I have shown enough variations; any deviation from the ideal are faulty.

As with the forelegs, the correct right-angled formation of the hindlegs should be easily gauged in the living dog by the width in profile shown in fig 5.14a as opposed to the narrow form in fig 5.14b. Bear in mind that the hindlegs are lighter in bone and the feet smaller than the front ones.

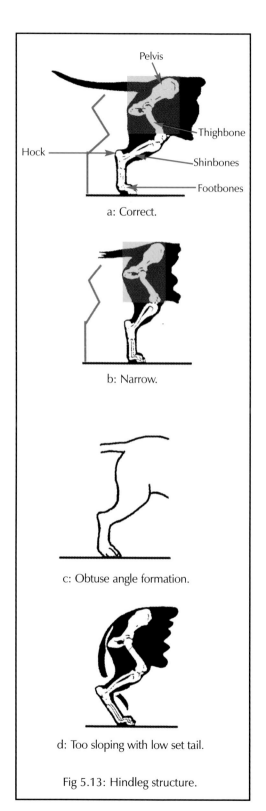

a: Correct.

b: Narrow.

c: Obtuse angle formation.

d: Too sloping with low set tail.

Fig 5.13: Hindleg structure.

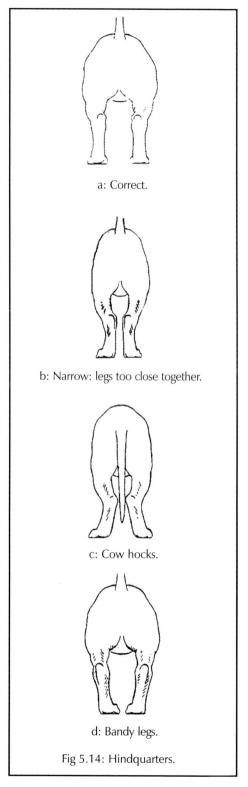

a: Correct.

b: Narrow: legs too close together.

c: Cow hocks.

d: Bandy legs.

Fig 5.14: Hindquarters.

Tail

Rule: Set on fairly high, strong and tapering, but not too long and not too much curved or carried too high.

Notes: If the tail is set too high it is liable to be hoisted over the back when the dog is excited. If set too low it may curl too much.

Ch Pipersvale Exclusive, owned and bred by Betty Munt.
Photo: John D Jackson

Coat and skin:
Smooth-haired variety

Rule: Short, dense and smooth, but strong. The hair on the underside of the tail coarse in texture, skin loose and supple.

Notes: This rule applies to the Smooth-coated only. The word loose in the last line is apt to be misleading. The skin should fit the body closely all over, but be elastic when handled.

For the coats on the Long and Wire-haired varieties, I quote from the German standard which is authoritative:

Coat and skin:
Long-haired variety

The soft, sleek, shining, often slightly waved hair should be longer under the neck, on the underside of the body, and especially on the ears and behind the legs, becoming pronounced where feathered; the hair should attain its greatest length on the underside of the tail. The hair should fall

Miniature Long: Bonnerhill Valentino at Denver,
bred by Eileen Falconer Douglas, owned by Sue Roberts.

beyond the lower edge of the ear. Short hair on this place (the ear), so-called leather ear, is not desirable.

Too luxurious a coat causes the Long-haired Dachshund to seem coarse, and masks the type. The coat should remind one of an Irish Setter, and should give the dog an elegant appearance. Too thick hair on paws, so-called mops, is inelegant and renders the animal unfit for use.

The tail is carried gracefully in prolongation of the spine, and it is here that the hair attains its greatest length, forming a veritable flag.

It is a fault if the hair is equally long all over the body, if it is too curly or too harsh, if the tail is lacking, or if there is a very pronounced parting on the back or a vigorous growth between the toes.

Colour of hair, nose and nails: exactly like the Short-haired Dachshund.

Coat and skin:
Wire-haired variety

With the exception of the jaw, eyebrows and ears, the whole body is covered with a completely even, wool-permeated undercoat, close-lying; and short, thick, rough coat, resembling that of the German Wirehaired Pointer. There should be a beard on the chin. The eyebrows are bushy. On the ears the hair is shorter than on the body; quite smooth, but nevertheless in conformity with the rest of the coat.

Hexie at 18 weeks.

The tail is robust, as thickly haired as possible, gradually diminishing, and without a tuft. The general arrangement of the hair should be such that the Rough-haired Dachshund, seen from a distance, resembles the Smooth-haired.

It is a fault if the texture of the hair is soft in general, if it is too short or too long in any particular place, if it sticks out irregularly in all directions, or if it is curly or wavy; a flag tail is also objectionable.

Colour of Hair, Nose, and Nails: All colours are admissible. White patches on the chest, though allowable, are not desirable.

Colour

Rule: Any colour. No white except spot on breast. Nose and nails should be black. In Red dogs a red nose is permissible, but not desirable. In Chocolates and Dapples the nose may be brown or flesh coloured. In Dapples large spots of colour are undesirable, and the dog should be evenly dappled all over.

Notes: Though colour is of minor importance to me, pure, rich colour adds much to the general appearance. Deep yellow (or Red as it is called) is preferable to a light washy yellow in Red dogs, and black or dark streaks are not desirable. In Black-and-tan dogs the tan markings should be a rich dark colour. In Chocolates the body colour should not be pale; a liver tone is best. Such colours were formerly referred to as Livers.

Black noses and nails are preferable in dogs of all colours. Red or flesh coloured noses are permissible but they detract somewhat from the general appearance by giving a softness to the expression.

Standard Long: Ch Dandydayo Kamand Maker, owned by Daniel Roberts and Margaret Swan.
Photo: Diane Pearce

Faults

Rule: In General Appearance, weak or deformed, too high or too low to ground; Ears set on too high or too low; Eyes too prominent; Muzzle too short or pinched, either undershot or overshot; Forelegs too crooked or with hare or terrier feet, or flat spread toes (flat-footed), out at elbows; Body with too much dip behind the shoulders; Loins weak or too arched; Chest too flat or too short; Hindquarters weak or cow-hocked; Hips higher than shoulders.

Notes: To this I must add a waddling gait in movement. The dog should move in an easy, gliding manner, straight ahead, and not roll from side to side like a ship in a rough sea.

6 Breeding - groundwork

While veterinary science has advanced greatly over the last decade, procreation and natural birth remain unchanged. Our research would not have been complete without considering the work of Captain Portman Graham who did so much to help novice and experienced breeders alike.

Procedure and custom

Certain unwritten laws have come to be recognised as accepted custom. Adherence to these represents the difference between a good reputation and a tarnished image. An immaculate reputation matters a great deal to serious breeders and exhibitors. To the novice breeder, who may commit a misdemeanour through ignorance, we offer this

chapter as a useful guideline. Breaking a contract or making a mistake in a pedigree can cause bad feeling and, in an extreme case, may even lead to censure by The Kennel Club.

The stud fee

This is a matter for negotiation between the stud dog's owner and the owner of the bitch seeking his service. It is impossible to state a uniform fee, although usually they are pretty uniform, with slight variation according to the quality and reputation of the dog. As general rule of thumb, consider the price of service by a particular stud to be in the region of the price of a puppy from the resulting litter. In addition to this, the escalation in veterinary fees, feeding costs, show entry fees and travel costs make it

Family likeness: Silver Splash Bonnerhill (dam – above) and Bonnerhill Valentino at Denver (son).

understandable that stud fees will rise from year to year.

Family likeness: Garthorn Griselda at Bonnerhill
(dam – above) and son.

It is to be expected that the cost of a stud service depends on the quality and popularity of the dog, taking into account his achievements and the quality of the progeny he sires. By becoming a champion he has proved himself typical of the breed, and the cost of a service from such a dog will be reflected in the fee. Such a dog is in great demand, so the owner of a multiple CC winner will not want to overwork his stud dog. At the same time, the dog will have to earn his keep. Although he is prepotent (capable of producing his own qualities when put to a large range of bitches), his services will be used less often, and probably to approved bitches only.

To approved bitches

It is a fallacy to suppose that a stud dog is totally responsible for the excellence of the progeny, or that because he is a champion his bloodline will automatically overcome all the faults of an inferior bitch. On the contrary, some really outstanding dogs have never sired a worthwhile specimen in the course of their career. The value of the stud dog lies in the quality of his progeny, not in the dog himself. It is therefore understandable that the stud dog's owner will want to heighten the dog's chances of success by making sure he is mated to good bitches. Both parents contribute their share of qualities to the offspring; hence the breeding dictum, only the best to the best. For this reason, the owner of a reliable, top-earning stud would be foolish to allow him to be used on any bitch of mediocre or inferior calibre.

A perfect example of a really fine stud dog with a knowledgeable and caring owner is the famous Int Ch Wingcrest Smart Alec, owned and bred by Mrs May Batterson-Webster. Smart Alec has a faultless pedigree (Int Ch Hobbithill Lorgan of Wingcrest ex Int Ch Likely Lass of Wingcrest). How could such a mating go wrong? Smart Alec was retired from the show ring to start his career as a top stud dog when he was just three-and-a-half years old.

Int Ch Wingcrest Smart Alec (Miniature Smooth), owned by May Batterson-Webster, third best stud for all breeds. From a drawing by Tracy White.

With 30 CCs to his credit he has sired more than 20 champions, winning his place in Dachshund history as third best stud dog for all breeds, with a handsome trophy to prove it.

An example of a highly approved bitch is black-and-tan Miniature Smooth-haired Ch D'Arisca Delicacy, bred by Mrs Lovaine Coxon. Delicacy has 16 CCs to her credit and has produced three beautiful litters.

Ch D'Arisca Delicacy. Photo: Trafford

After each litter she has returned to the ring and delighted everyone with her consistent wins. In 1996 she again proved her quality by winning the Veteran Class at Crufts. Her line continues: her son D'Arisca Ambrose, championship winner in many continental countries, is training for his working title, which will make him an international champion and a European champion. Here in Great Britain, Delicacy's daughter Ch D'Arisca Candice is delighting all who are privileged to see her strutting her stuff in the ring. Ch D'Arisca Delicacy is the daughter of Ch/Ir Ch Pipersvale Smart Alec out of Dalegarth Della, which again proves the point.

Ch Pipersvale Pina Colada. Photo: Anne Roslin-Williams

Not every puppy from such matings has that little bit extra needed to make a champion, and it has to be said that every Dachshund is an individual. The dog must have panache and the temperament to enjoy showing. Also, the finest Dachshund can be ruined by bad handling. In the right hands a plain dog can be made to look good; in the wrong hands, a perfect specimen can look terrible and behave most dreadfully. Anyone privileged to watch Lovaine Coxon filling the eye and commanding the ring at Crufts with Ch D'Arisca Candice in 1996 was witness to an experienced handler demonstrating a perfect balance between Dachshund and handler; they were in complete accord.

A further example of the advisability of a stud dog being available to approved bitches only was Ch Pipersvale Pina Colada, the very fine Miniature Dachschund bred and owned by Mrs Betty Munt. Pina Colada had an incredible 70 CCs and sired at least 15 champions. When put to Jarad Blue Moon, owned and bred by Mrs J CLiff, he sired such outstanding Dachshunds as: Ch Pipersvale Chocolat Royal, Ch Jarad Chocolate Surprise at Pipersvale and Ch Pipersvale A Trifle Tipsy.

Pipersvale Pina Colada went on to win BIS at the Southern Counties championship Show, beating all comers of every breed; a feat later matched by his daughter, Chocolate Surprise at the Midland Counties Championship Show. In all, more than 27 champions have graced Betty Munt's home.

I think these examples make our point: careful and selective breeding is well worth the cost of a stud, provided that the bitch is worthy of the proposed sire.

Breeding terms
Breeding terms can cover a multitude of prerequisites and restrictions and I cannot say that I favour such arrangements except in exceptional circumstances. Many a friendship has been ruined by a misunderstanding of such terms. If an agreement is made, a contract must be drawn up in duplicate and signed by both parties, a copy to be retained by each. In the event of a disagreement or any non-compliance, written proof of the original intention is on hand. The document should cover all likely contingencies so that there can be no excuse for acrimonious argument.

For instance, in the case of a *puppy in lieu of a service fee*, an agreement should be drawn up in advance covering the eventuality that only one puppy is born or has survived the whelping. Strictly speaking, the puppy belongs to the owner of the stud dog, unless different arrangements have been made. Disappointing as this may be, you must consider that the stud dog owner has suspended payment and is in business: neither sentiment nor friendship pays the rent.

Again, agreement should previously have been reached as to who should have first choice of the litter.

If no puppies arrive, the service fee for the dog is still due. This hurdle is sometimes overcome by agreeing that, in the event of no puppies being produced, a further service is offered on the bitch's next season, with the same agreement applying. If the bitch whelps a litter then the dog will have fulfilled his part, but if the whelps should die before the owner of the dog receives his or her puppy the bitch owner's side of the bargain has not been fulfilled. In these instances it can be agreed beforehand that, if for any reason no whelp is forthcoming in lieu of the fee, either the fee or part of the fee should subsequently be paid to the stud dog owner. Alternatively, the same conditions can be imposed on the bitch owner, and a puppy shall be due from a subsequent season and litter.

These are examples of various forms of agreement, and are not meant to imply any hard or fast rules. The actual terms for the parties concerned should be worked out by mutual agreement. Overall, it has to be said that it is less complicated to pay for the service outright. Otherwise, remember that written agreements lead to goodwill all round, because everyone knows exactly where they stand; oral agreements are hazardous, often causing bad feeling, disappointment and resentment.

Stud fees

Stud fees: what exactly are you paying for? This often confuses the novice breeder.

If the stud dog is a proven sire, payment for his service is due irrespective of a result: you are paying for the service. Moreover, the fee is due in advance, before the mating. It should be understood that once the bitch has been served, the 'goods' have been delivered.

The owner of the bitch should be allowed to see the chosen stud dog prior to the mating as evidence that he is fit and well. It is sometimes better if the bitch owner is not at the actual mating, as strangers may put a stud dog off his task. However, once the mating has been effected and a tie has resulted, the stud dog owner should call in the owner of the bitch to provide proof of a bona fide service. An erectile dog who has fully penetrated the bitch and shows signs that he is 'spent' is evidence that the bitch has been mated.

If no actual 'tie' has been effected the stud dog owner has to decide honestly whether the mating has been adequate to the purpose and he or she is justified in keeping the fee. Strictly speaking, a tie is not always essential for a successful mating, so an honest assessment must be made as to how likely the mating is to be productive.

Exchanging papers

Copies of pedigrees should be exchanged as soon as negotiations for stud begin. For obvious reasons it is important that these pedigrees are compatible. If the user has not seen the dog then the stud owner may forward a photograph of the prospective sire, and it is quite courteous to ask for its return.

After the service the stud dog owner should sign and date the (blue) *Kennel Club Application for a Litter Registration by the Breeder (Form 1)*. These are available from The Kennel Club. The signed form should then be given to the bitch's owner. The blue form is written confirmation of a mating to a particular dog and no litter can be registered without it. All such forms should be applied for in good time to allow for their delivery.

The bitch's owner should also receive a copy of the sire's pedigree if one has not been sent with the initial enquiry and a receipt for all monies paid to the stud dog owner.

The word pedigree implies an accurate genealogical record. Many breeders study these lines very carefully and the slightest error will soon be picked up. If you are in any doubt as to one or more of the dogs listed on your pedigree the easiest solution is to apply for a copy of the official pedigree from The Kennel Club. There are cases where mistakes can occur through negligence. However, a small minority of scoundrels fake pedigrees intentionally to place a higher value on their litters. Our safeguard is The Kennel Club, which censures such people very severely, but if you keep careful records yourself the chances of anything more than a slight spelling mistake are slim.

A word about advertising: do be correct in everything you claim. Gross exaggeration harms your reputation, and there are laws to protect the consumer. There will be very little about your dog that knowledgeable breeders don't already know, and who needs a bad reputation?

The brood bitch

Let us first dismiss the myth that unless every bitch has at least one litter she is somehow being deprived of an inherent need. This is not true.

Unlike *Homo sapiens*, other species of animals only conceive when in season, and dogs are no exception. In the periods between seasons there is no possibility of the bitch being mated. The instinct to mate is usually short lived, and in the bitch it is limited to three or four days during a longer period of about 21 days known as her season or heat. At this time the bitch may flirt outrageously with other animals, not necessarily of her own kind.

Psychologically, this flirting often sends messages to her body that she has been successfully mated, although in fact she has not. Her body and psyche may take over and starts preparing her for motherhood, triggering the whole biological process and resulting in what is known as a phantom, or false, pregnancy. The results are often quite startling. She may put on weight, become 'broody' and display swollen, milk-giving mammary glands. By all means consult your vet, who may suggest that you let things run their course or advise hormone treatment and tablets to disperse the milk. Whatever the advice, be assured that this bewildering phenomenon will not harm the bitch and she will eventually revert to normal.

Taking a litter from a pet bitch should be thought over very carefully. One rarely awakens one morning to find a basket full of delightful puppies that the bitch has produced all by herself in the night. To the amateur, however well-intentioned, breeding is a serious business best left to those who know what they are doing. Having said that, we all have to start somewhere.

For the novice breeder the pitfalls are many. It is a stressful business, a time for great anxiety, anxiety which will inevitably be transferred to the bitch. Not all Dachshunds whelp easily – the incidence of Caesarean section is quite high compared to other breeds.

Neither is it necessarily a profitable venture. The initial stud fee, care of the bitch, injections and veterinary fees, possible surgery, extra heating, the feeding of mother and puppies: all these add to the expense. Those who merely wish to breed from a bitch to get another puppy are strongly advised to buy one in. To newcomers deeply interested in furthering the breed who want to own a show dog they have bred themselves, I repeat: we all have to start somewhere.

Choosing a brood bitch

All other breeders should be reminded that the strength of any kennel lies in the quality of its bitches, and a mediocre bitch will rarely produce anything better than herself. Therefore, before buying a brood bitch, her looks and pedigree must be examined with great care.

Your well-set-up bitch may have been the only decent product of a particular litter. Conversely, she may have been the poorest specimen, with a stunning pedigree. Always consider the bitch and her pedigree together.

Ch Marictur Beau Mezzo, a fourth-generation champion bitch.

It is possible to have a very sound bitch with no obvious faults, not particularly outstanding herself, but whose pedigree suggests she is carrying the right genes. If so, bear in mind that it is not uncommon for a plain bitch (for want of a better description) with the right pedigree behind her, when taken to a proven stud, consistently to produce wonderful puppies. But if you take a mediocre bitch with an uninspiring pedigree to a top stud, do not expect the puppies from this mating to inherit all the sire's qualities with none of the dam's shortcomings. That is akin to mating Prince Charming with one of the Ugly Sisters! Each parent contributes equally to the quality of the offspring, and at best it is a gamble. No one can predict what bad faults will be dominant, or how the puppies will end up. What's more, it does not stop there: doubled-up faults will almost certainly be passed on to the next generation, and so on.

Symptoms of ovulation

The *season* or *heat* is easily recognised. Most bitches come into season at about six month, but this is only a general rule of thumb. Some bitches, particularly in the miniature varieties, come into season at 10-monthly, or even yearly, intervals.

The signs are easily recognised. The earliest indication is the enlargement of the vulva. Very often, before the owner is aware of the signs, a dog shows indications of becoming sexually aware of the bitch. This state might continue for several days before the next definite sign.

The next stage is a thick, dark red discharge. The owner must make a careful note of the date as it is from the showing of colour that the optimum date for mating is calculated. The period of ovulation lasts anything from 21 days to (exceptionally) a month.

It is normally around the 10th day that the tissue of the vulva becomes looser and much softer and the colour of the discharge lightens to faint pink, gradually becoming colourless by the 14th to 16th day. Remember that the bitch is not necessarily matable throughout the whole of this period. The term *ready* refers to when she is willing to consort with the dog and invites intercourse. The main sign is her readiness to stand for the dog. She will unashamedly flirt by thrusting her bottom at him and curling her tail to the side. This may be tested by the owner gently touching her vulva. When she is ready she will curl her tail instinctively. The period during which a bitch is ready can vary. In some cases she will only stand for a dog during a period of a few hours; in others she will be ready from two to six days. In exceptional cases she may be ready for a whole fortnight. This makes it very important for owners to keep records.

As a general rule it is rare for a bitch to be mated before the 9th day or after the 15th day, but there have been extreme cases where a mating effected as late as the 18th day has resulted in a litter. As a general rule the 11th day is accepted as the most suitable, but each season is unique and the bitch should be observed closely during the season, particularly if arrangements have been made for the services of a stud dog. If the discharge ceases early and there are indications that the vulva is shrinking before the expected date, fresh arrangements must be made hastily.

It should also be stressed that, even after a successful mating, the bitch remains vulnerable for several days. Segregation must be maintained for her full 21 days and not relaxed until all traces of the oestrus have cleared. If a bitch has been served by more than one dog in the same heat the names of all the dogs must be given when the litter is registered with The Kennel Club

During the whole period of oestrus the bitch causes sexual stimulation in any dog. This is induced by a discharge from the bitch to which a dog will be receptive. It is not wise to keep both bitch and dog in the house at this time, even if the bitch is segragated from the dog. The smell, which cannot be detected by humans, will pervade the house. It is kinder all round to house the bitch in an outside kennel with a small run.

The strain on a male is quite considerable and may cause undue harm to his nervous system. Novice owners are sometimes quite startled to discover that their otherwise chirpy little dog has become lethargic and dour, his interest in food fading and his weight dropping alarmingly. It explains why some breeders keep either brood bitches only or stud dogs only. If there is a problem with segregation this is a far safer option.

In the event of an accidental mating a veterinary surgeon can administer an injection that will abort the conception if administered within 12–24 hours of mating.

A question which often arises is, if there has been an unsuitable mating, possibly with a mongrel, will the bitch be ruined by the production of unsuitable puppies? The answer is an unequivocal *No*. While the puppies will be valueless as pedigree stock, subsequent litters will not be affected. When mated to a pedigree dog of her own breed she will produce perfectly fine puppies.

Number and frequency of litters

Quote: *The Kennel Club will not accept an application to register a litter if the dam has already whelped six litters, or if the dam has reached the age of eight years, although in the latter case special consideration will only be given, provided application for permission is made before the mating.*

If a bitch comes into season before she is 12 months old it is unwise to mate her on her first season. It is better to wait until her next season, when she will be more mature both physically and temperamentally. The exception is for Miniatures, where whelping is generally a little more difficult than for Standards. If a bitch is very late starting her first season, not doing so until 12–18 months of age, she may be mated on her first season.

Any owner who loves his or her bitches and respects their welfare allows them to be mated only every other season. However, an exceptionally strong, healthy bitch can be mated twice in three seasons; that is, if she is allowed to have litters on two successive seasons, she must be rested for the next. If a bitch has been a maiden for three or four years there is considerable risk of her having a difficult time whelping. This is often the case when an exhibitor is campaigning the bitch, showing her intensively in an attempt to make her up to champion. Some older bitches slip quite happily into motherhood with no problems but, unfortunately, this is not always the case.

It is understandable that owners of successful bitches may be reluctant to forego the limelight, and that they will want to continue successful lines; what is not fair is that they should want to have their cake and eat it. Gaining the triple crown, those valuable three CCs that make a dog a champion, is no mean feat. Two or three more are evidence that it was no fluke, and this is both understandable and desirable. But campaigning any exhibit in the endless pursuit of CCs, particularly a bitch from whom the owner wishes to breed, is selfish. Perhaps it is more understandable with a dog at public stud – after all a stud in the limelight will be much in demand. However, a bitch, particularly a Miniature, may run into problems if first mated after the age of three.

The stud dog

When to start

A successful stud dog must be trained to combine business with pleasure. A dog who does not gain his first experience while still relatively young will be difficult to make into an intelligent stud dog. If he has not been put to a bitch until he is three or four years old he will probably have no idea of what is expected of him. The best age to start his training is about 10 months. He should then not be expected to serve again for at least another two months. After that, he should serve one bitch a month until he is at least 18 months old.

This is only a guide. To a robust and virile dog aged more than 15 months the occasional additional bitch would not be detrimental, but to overuse a dog of less than 18 months is to weaken him and, if carried to excess, to ruin him. The starting age of 10 months need not be slavishly adhered to, but is quoted as the optimum age. Earlier services are not necessarily bad provided that the dog is well rested before he tries to repeat the process.

A successful stud: Ch Bothlyn Mastercraftsman.

Youth to experience

As a general principle, take an old brood bitch to a young, inexperienced dog. Conversely, let an older stud dog serve a young maiden bitch. The result is generally larger sized litters with no degeneracy. It is not always sound to take a very old bitch to a very old stud dog. The size of the litter is invariably diminished, and deterioration in the progeny usually results. Frequently only one puppy of exceptional size arrives and this is sometimes very dangerous to the bitch at whelping time.

When to stop

Let us consider the age up to which a dog can be profitably used at stud with a reasonable chance of the bitch's owner having an honest deal and a fair prospect of a worthwhile litter. This varies with individual dogs, so no strict rules can be set down. However, as a general guide it can be said that a 10-year-old stud has certainly aged. If he has been used extensively over the years, in regard to sexual competence he is older than a dog of the same age who has been used less often. Beyond the age of 10 the activity of the sperm diminishes and smaller, degenerate stock should be expected. Dogs of 12 and over have been used, but these are exceptional. A 12-year-old dog is equal to a man in his 80s. Think about it: there have to be limits.

Genetic factors

For the owner of a bitch contemplating mating her on her next season, compatibility must be a consideration. Having made your choice, contact the owner of your chosen stud and ask permission to use his services. If you have never seen the dog in person it might be worth asking for an appointment to see him. Do not take your bitch to the nearest dog simply because it is handy and less bother. A reputable stud is well worth the travel.

There are three options: Line-breeding, in-breeding, and out-crossing. Each option has its exponents and opponents!

- **Line-breeding** is the breeding of a bitch to a dog descended from the same ancestors. Examples would be half-brother to half-sister, grandson to grandmother, niece to uncle or aunt to nephew.
- **In-breeding** is breeding to close relatives: father to daughter, mother to son, or full brother to full sister.
- **Out-cross** breeding is breeding a bitch to a line with no, or only a few, mutual ancestors.

Of all the choices, **line-breeding** is safest for the novice. With such a system the gene pool will be larger and uniformity of type is assured. Faults are less fixed and general type is more likely to continue. When breeding for a certain type, the process takes much longer.

In-breeding, if practised at all, is something best left to the more experienced breeder. There are those who persist in likening the practice to the laws governing human beings. Antagonists declare, with no evidence to prove the point, that the practice inevitably leads to imperfections. The truth is that in-breeding intensifies good and bad points by doubling them up. Both dogs contribute equally to the genes of the puppy, so the puppy inherits those points, good and bad, already present. In in-breeding they are present in such strength that they often outweigh the inherited factors from other dogs in the pedigree. It is inevitable that small faults, otherwise dormant but still being carried, will surface more quickly. Few litters are faultless even with ideal parents, and not all puppies have potential show quality, but with in-breeding failures are more likely to happen. What is good will likely be very good, but the percentages will be against you and doubled-up faults will be passed on to future generations. It follows that only perfect puppies should be bred from; all others should be considered pet quality. Some breeders advocate the ruthless culling of such offspring, but I would rather withhold registration and home them in pet homes. This is a controversial subject, so I hasten to add that this is my personal opinion.

Out-crossing, even with the backing of two very fine pedigrees, is a gamble, albeit an educated one. It is impossible to forecast the outcome with any degree of accuracy. When breeding for a particular type this might take a long time, possibly years. However, if you keep only the best and then line-breed, a general type will eventually appear. This is why most breeders will look for a deciding factor in the pedigree, one that carries one or more shared ancestors of the type required.

Breeding for colour
*Many thanks to **Pauline Anderson** for her help with this section.*

The Standards states: *All colours are allowed but (except in dapples which should be evenly marked all over) no white permissible, save for a small patch on chest which is permissible but not desirable. Nose and nails black in all colours except chocolate/tan and chocolate/dapple, where brown is permissible.*

That's clear enough, but how do we get the colours we are aiming for?

Colour is inherited and, in breeding one particular colour to another, we must try for those colours that are ascendant. For instance, red is dominant to black-and-tan, while black-and-tan is dominant to chocolate; in other words, the dominant colours are more powerful or prominent than the competition.

If we breed two reds together their offspring will be red; two black-and-tans together produce black-and-tan puppies.

That seems quite simple enough until we consider the different colours behind each pedigree: each dog is capable of carrying colour.

To explain *carrying* we must explain the laws governing the formulation of heredity characteristics, known as the *Mendelian* principles. Gregor Johann Mendel, Abbot of Brunn, discovered these laws while experimenting with the cross-fertilisation of garden produce. This led to the formulation of the *laws of heredity* showing that certain characteristics, such as height and colour, depend on the presence of hereditary determining genes, which may be either recessive or dominant. So if we consider that each litter of puppies has two parents, and that each parent is capable of contributing different characteristics, it is easy to understand that the resulting puppies have something from each parent. With this in mind we can understand why different coloured puppies can be produced from the same litter. The same rule applies to man: it is perfectly acceptable that brothers and sisters may have different hair or eye colouring depending on the recessive genes they carry.

It has to be said that breeding for a particular colour is more successful when line-breeding principles are adopted, so that the particular colour required is taken and bred to that colour. We can therefore reasonably expect red/red to produce red, black-and-tan/black-and-tan to produce black-and-tan and chocolate/chocolate to produce chocolate. When considering those dogs carrying a different colour we must decide which colour is dominant.

Red is dominant to black-and-tan, while both red and black-and-tan are dominant to chocolate. But brindle is dominant to both red and black-and-tan. The odd guy out is chocolate: most colours are dominant to chocolate but, provided that the colour is rich and deep, chocolate may be bred to chocolate to produce chocolate. The danger here is that, to keep the eye and nail colouring dark (at least, brown), the occasional mating back to a black-and-tan is essential. Without reverting back to a strong colour, such as black-and-tan, the strength of colour in chocolates will diminish.

Three champions owned by Sue Roberts:
red, dapple and black-and-tan.

The same may be said for the continual mating of red to red. A clear or *Schneid* red (named after Monsieur Schneidig) is a highly desirable colour, being a true red without any black hair at all. This can be produced by mating red to red, but not to the extent that the original colour becomes pale and faded. To keep the depth of colour acceptable, black-and-tan matings must be introduced at healthy intervals.

Of all the colours, black-and-tan is the stabilising colour. Without its modifying influence many true colours become pale and washed-out, eventually producing the dreaded pale eye and nose features.

There are no problems when mating two rich colours together, but deterioration is only to be expected if you breed continually from pale and dull colours and animals of the same pigmentation. This can be said of both reds and chocolates. Immediately any of the whelps show signs of becoming neutralised the stabilising influence of a black-and-tan should be considered.

Although it is no longer permissible in the United Kingdom to breed different varieties together, it is perfectly permissible to breed different colours together. As with all things, there are unwritten rules governing the practice. A much-argued point is what happens when you take a red to a chocolate. As red is the dominant colour, the likelihood is that you will have all red puppies. If the red is carrying black-and-tan there is a possibility of having puppies of both red and black-and-tan, but very rarely will you get a chocolate.

The problems with such a mating may come about later, when the resulting puppies in their turn are mated to chocolates, dogs carrying chocolate. The risk is that some of the resulting puppies may be born with light eyes and pale noses. Dark eyes and noses are dominant to light, but light pigmentation can occur, even when the progeny are taken to colours other than chocolate.

When you take Mendel's law of dominance or his statistics of genetic chance into account it is reasonable to assume some expectancy when breeding sensibly for a particular colour. However, the resulting colours can prove disappointing when the pedigree is not studied closely. While there are expectations, there can be no hard and fast guarantees.

We may be certain of the colour of the two dogs in a particular mating, and may even know something of the colours behind their pedigrees, but nature can play some pretty naughty tricks. Somewhere in every dog's extraction can lie an anterior factor which may prove dominant. This may be better demonstrated, particularly in Miniature Long-haired Dachshunds, when a latent disease like GPRA (Generalised Progressive Retinal Atrophy) is present in a dog or bitch's pedigree. The dog itself may be free of the disease, but the danger lies in the possibility that it may be a carrier and that its progeny may develop the disease from one of the ancestors in its pedigree. A harrowing thought, but it does serve to demonstrate that the colours behind a dog may prove to be dominant.

There are instances when a breeder has been pleasantly surprised when a colour that has been recessive for several generations suddenly pops out unexpectedly in a litter. It is usually just one puppy carrying the colour, but it can cause some head-scratching. I had a Miniature Long-haired silver dapple bitch who, in each of her litters, even though taken to a very strong and dominantly black-and-tan dog, produced one chocolate dapple puppy, and beautiful they were too. Research proved that there was just one chocolate dog in her pedigree – six generations back.

Much the same rule applies to Long-haired Dachshunds as applies to Smooths. The expected colours are the same, with the exception of dapples.

The dapple markings in the show Dachshund need to be even. This means that the base colour should be silver-grey and the patches made up of equal patches of black and silver hairs. No part of the body, limbs or head should show dense or unbroken areas of black. The tan markings are usually on the head and legs. In the chocolate dapple the under-colour is a mixture of chocolate and silver hairs and the patches are chocolate. No white is should be present apart from a small patch on the chest, which is permissible but not desirable. Again, the nose and nails should be black, although in the chocolate dapple they may be brown. On the other hand, the eyes may be dark, brown or wall. *Wall* means that the eye may be the colour of the surrounding patch on that part of the face. In other words, if the patch around one eye is black and silver the eye should be dark on that side; if the patch on the other side is lighter the eye may be a lighter shade, possibly blue. It is not unusual for dapples to have two different eyecolourings.

It is also permissible for chocolate and chocolate dapples to have brown noses and nails, the darker the tone the better. Pale or pink noses,eyes or nails are not permissible: they must be brown or wall, wall meaning blue or lighter tone.

Breeding for dapple is not difficult; the difficulty lies in breeding a dapple with the correct markings, and this can a very 'hit-and-miss' affair. Dapple will eventually appear when a dapple dog or bitch is taken to a whole-colour. Dapples with wrong markings are usually sold to pet homes. Dapple to dapple produces dapple, and possibly also whole-colour, depending on what is behind the pedigree. However, no black-and-tan can carry the genes for dapple markings even when bred from a dapple mating. Chocolate to dapple produces chocolate dapple, silver dapple if there is a percentage of silver dapple in the genes, and whole-colour such as chocolate. Again, it must be stressed that it is not easy to breed a perfectly marked dapple.

In the past it was extremely difficult for a dapple to succeed in the show ring when competing with other colours. Perhaps because all dapples trace back to a common ancestor, many of them in the past shared the same faults in construction. This was mainly evident in the 1950s, 1960s and early 1970s but, as with evolution in all things, as a result of careful out-crossing to other colours, well-bred examples of specimens more representative of the breed, the dapple has now come into its own and we have some very fine examples who have gained their well-deserved triple crown.

Tanska La Blonde, bred by Fay Skanta.

Cream Long-hairs: (left to right) Devonwood Solo Adventurer, Weaverbird Fly Home at Devonwood and Devonwood Cream Tease; all owned by Pauline Anderson.

Cream and shaded cream Dachshunds, particularly in Miniature Long-hairs, have become very popular, and many of the principles adopted for the breeding of dapples apply equally to creams. Cream taken to cream produces a higher percentage of cream; taken to a whole colour the percentage is lower and the points are darker. Cream taken to red produces red, cream and golden cream. Cream taken to black-and-tan produces a percentage of cream, black-and-cream, and shaded cream. As with dapples, the points should be dark, but continual in-breeding to cream tends to lighten the shades.

The photograph reproduced above, by kind permission of Pauline Anderson of the Devonwood affix, illustrates perfectly the range of cream and shaded cream in the ideally bred Long-haired Dachshund. Also the photograph opposite of two of her cream Longs as puppies, Devonwood Sophie's Choice and Devonwood Lady Daisy, illustrates perfectly the change of colour from puppy to adult coats. Here I quote Mrs Anderson: *The photographs of the two puppies illustrate the changing colours of creams. Creams can be actually born cream, but are usually born a sort of brown or greyish black. It takes about eight weeks for the black to disappear and the cream to emerge, although some creams retain a saddle of black until they are approximately 16 weeks old. The paler creams are usually a 'muffin' colour until about six months old. The Cornish ice-cream colour, or 'lemon' cream, is usually present at an early age and just comes through gradually until all the black eventually disappears. The two ladies in the picture are 'lemon' cream, taken at two weeks old. You will see that they have already shed some of their black hairs and the cream is coming through. At the time of writing this they are ten months old and a beautifully clear 'lemon' cream.*

Colour is very much a case of individual preference. Of course the more flashy colours will catch the eye, and this can, and often does, bring about bad judging, in which judges award for colour rather than conformation, construction and movement. It has to be said that no dog should be considered for a high award on coat or colour alone: what lies beneath the coat is of paramount importance. It should be born in mind that, just as an experienced handler can show a dog to its ultimate advantage, so can a coat hide a myriad of faults from an inexperienced judge. To the discerning and experienced onlooker, this factor will soon become apparent, and such judges will find a depletion in the numbers of exhibitors willing to show under them. Great care should be taken not to be blinded by colour. This applies equally when buying a puppy: construction and soundness must take priority over colour. Fortunately we have breeders such as Mrs Anderson, whose Devonwood affix is in itself a guarantee of soundness. Again, we stress that colour is a matter of preference; all colours are permissible, barring white.

Cream Long-hair puppies: Devonwood Sophie's Choice (left) and Devonwood Lady Daisy; owned by Pauline Anderson.

7 Breeding - practicalities

The service

No breeder can render adequate assistance to a mating without knowing at least something of the anatomical make-up of the dog and bitch.

Anatomy of the dog

The normal dog has two testicles contained in the scrotum. These manufacture the seminal fluid containing millions of spermatozoa (sperm). This fluid makes its way via a cord to the penis. In the anterior part of the penis is a bone which varies in size according to the breed. The organ is protected by a sheath of skin, technically called the prepuce, and this is loosely attached at the bulb. The only parts of the organ which need concern the owner of the stud dog are the front part, which is composed of erectile tissue ending in a fine-pointed end, and behind this a rounded bulb, also composed of erectile tissue.

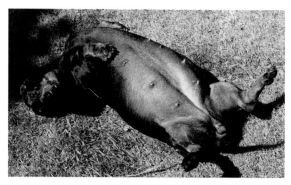

Ch Marictur Modesty Blaise (8½ weeks pregnant) enjoying a stretch.

It is due to this structure that the tie can occur. From the stud dog owner's point of view, this tie is important. From the bulb two large veins connect to the back of the penis where there are two muscles. The organ functions as follows:

Ch Marictur Modesty Blaise in show condition.

- Sexual excitement enables the organ to become erect, allowing it to penetrate the female passage.
- Sensory frictional nerve impulses induce the ejection of the fluid.
- The muscles simultaneously compress the veins, causing them to become engorged in the bulb.

Once inside the female passage the bulb becomes very congested and swollen, causing the female passage to become completely locked around it. This condition may last for a period ranging from two minutes to an hour. The organ remains entirely flexible throughout this procedure and while ejaculation is taking place. While in position the dog can, and should, be turned around to face in the opposite direction.

Anatomy of the bitch

The external genitals of the bitch (the vulva) is often referred to as the lips of the vagina. This is a thickened, fleshy orifice which faces downward. Internally the vagina is long and narrows as it progresses into the body. The vulva also houses erectile tissue (the glans clitoris) which corresponds to that of the dog. This is what induces the bitch's acceptance of the dog.

The vaginal passage ends in a constriction as it emerges into the uterus, or womb, in other words at the cervix or neck of the womb.

The uterus is comparatively short, about one third of the length of the vagina. It is divided into a V shape, into two horns which go forward on each side in the abdomen for a considerable distance. The uterine horns are practically straight, narrow in diameter, being approximately six times the length of the body of the uterus. Each uterine horn culminates in a structure known as the ovary, which is smaller in size than the body of the uterus. Then, leading from each ovary is a tube known as the fallopian tube. The purpose of the ovaries is to produce ova, or eggs, which pass down the fallopian tube to each horn of the womb. The transfer of the ova from the ovaries to the womb takes place only during the bitch's seasons.

During mating the ova is pierced by innumerable sperms, but only one is successful. The cell of the ovum and the cell of the sperm then divide. The whole process is known as the fertilisation of the ovum. The fertilised ova attach themselves to the membranous walls of each horn of the womb. The unfertilised ova pass out as a mucous discharge. During the ensuing weeks, known as the gestation period, further development from the two original sex cells continues. Their fusion forms an embryo or foetus. Gestation normally lasts for 63 days, at the end of which the foetus is a fully-developed puppy.

Behaviour of the stud dog

Dogs are as variable in their behaviour and attitudes to sex as their human counterparts. With this in mind perhaps we should explain some of the types in general terms.

Macho guy: He is the no-nonsense, butch type. He knows exactly what the bitch is there for and gets to work immediately without worrying about her, mounting her with no time wasted on preliminaries. If the bitch is ready he will have no problem penetrating.

The dangers are that the dog may be a trifle too insensitive. Care must be taken with a highly-strung, nervous bitch. If the bitch is uncooperative the dog should be restrained a little. Hold him on a lead and encourage him to be a little more gentle. If a macho dog is allowed to serve a nervous bitch with no consideration for her fear, she will tighten her muscles instead of relaxing them and penetration by the dog will be difficult, not to say painful, for her. She will snap and bite, doing all in her power to avoid the union by turning and pulling herself away, or even by rolling on the ground.

Gently restraining the dog and patiently soothing the bitch will bring about a successful union. Remember that assistance must not be hurried and great patience is needed, especially with a maiden bitch.

Average fellow: This chap takes things in his stride and is neither aggressive nor too premature. Quite often he does not approach the bitch immediately, but sits and watches her, thinking things over. In his own good time he approaches her and demonstrates his affection by nuzzling his head against her and licking her ears. He often smells and licks her vulva. He is not put off by the flirtatious and coquettish behaviour of a ready bitch, who may run around, stand, and then run around again – in fact, he often joins in, playing up to her.

Provided that the assistants do not try to hurry either the dog or the bitch, this can be regarded as the normal, straightforward mating. Owners of such a dogs can think themselves fortunate. Although a bit slow, this type of dog makes a sure and sound stud.

Shy type: Some dogs are naturally shy and can be overawed by the whole proceedings. If the bitch becomes skittish and chases such a nervous fellow he will probably run away. However, when a degree of excitement is created he will mount diffidently, only to drop away again.

This type is completely the opposite of 'macho guy'. Even when mounted and doing his utmost to serve the bitch he is easily put off. If she is snappy and turns her head, showing her teeth or growling as some do, his ardour evaporates. He drops away and won't 'play' again.

When this type of dog eventually penetrates the bitch he must be pushed firmly up to her and kept there; otherwise his nervousness will cause him to slip out again. Even when he has tied and is functioning he may be apprehensive. When turned he tries to come apart, wriggling and sometimes causing the bitch pain.

With this type there is undoubtedly a need for two handlers – one to steady and soothe the bitch and one to hold the dog firmly, but not forcibly.

This type may improve with training but will never become a confident stud dog. His first few matings should be arranged with ready, and cooperative bitches. However coquettish the bitch may be, this type of dog never responds to natural mating, so don't waste your time by expecting him to behave normally and don't give the bitch an opportunity to flirt too openly. She should be held stationary, facing front. One handler should place a hand on each side of her head and neck, grasping her reasonably firmly so that she cannot turn round or even move from this position. This is the handler's job throughout the whole proceedings: to keep the bitch still and prevent her from turning her head.

If she is ready, cooperative and curling her tail and the dog is stimulated, in due course he will attempt a tentative mounting. Let him do this a few times to stimulate him further.

The other helper should be alert, watching for the first actual negotiation, and then firmly press the dog closely to the bitch, holding him there. As exhausting as it is, with this type it is not advisable to attempt to turn the dog too soon. Often it is better not to do so at all.

If the dog is too diffident even to mount and attempt penetration himself he may need some guidance. His attitude is not due to lack of instinct, which may be quite keen, but to lack of confidence.

Disinterested male: Some dogs are lethargic and quite unintelligent as far as mating is concerned. They are similar to 'shy type', the only difference being the sexual instinct of 'shy type' is normal. 'Disinterested male' is the most difficult type to deal with, but fortunately he is in a very small minority.

With these animals it is often necessary to resort to hand stimulation to get them going. If the response results in erectile tissue the penis should be guided into the vulva and the dog held into the bitch. It has been known for such disinterested males eventually to become quite sound studs.

Behaviour of the bitch

Bitches have considerably fewer types than their male counterparts. As long as they are ready and curling their tails most stand quite willingly. A bitch has a much stronger sexual instinct than a young male, although bitches seldom exhibit instinct at any other time.

Some maiden bitches are frightened. In such cases, understanding and firm encouragement must be used. The maiden bitch must have time to settle before being introduced to the dog. Her fear is partly due to the presence of strangers and strange surroundings. Few are inherently snappy or vicious but they can be put off by 'macho type' who is rough. Great care must be employed to curb the enthusiasm of such a dog without destroying his natural ability. Second and subsequent matings with fearful bitches are usually much easier.

On introducing the bitch to the dog you must observe and quickly decide how she is going to react. If she is playful and coquettish you can expect her to behave like the majority of bitches; and in this case the mating should be quite straightforward. On the other hand, if she runs away or tries to hide, snarls or shows her teeth, she is afraid. This will not be overcome by leaving the dog and the bitch together in the hope that they will strike up a friendship.

When the bitch is one day before or one day after her best day she is still perfectly mateable. Generally speaking bitches are more willing to stand after rather than before. In these cases the bitch is frequently uncooperative, unresponsive, snappy and resentful of the dog, in much the same manner as the frightened bitch. The handling must be the same: a soothing tone and gentle coaxing, using her name, but a degree of firmness in making her stand. It may be advisable to muzzle her if she shows signs that she might bite or damage the stud dog. A length of 5cm-wide crepe bandage works very well. Folded in half, width ways, and placed across the muzzle, it is then crossed beneath the jaws and brought up to be tied behind the head.

The mating

The right day having been estimated, the owner of the bitch should inform the stud owner that the bitch is on her way. It is usual for the bitch to be taken to the dog. Particularly if she has had a long journey, the bitch should be given time to acclimatise herself to her surrounding. There should be no rushing. If she is to stay over, she should be given a light meal and a drink and be introduced to her quarters. It is sometimes helpful to allow her to have her own blanket, or something that smells familiar.

The condition of the bitch should be a matter of personal pride. She should be bathed, brushed and groomed. It is the height of bad form to present a bitch who is in a dirty condition. She should be obviously healthy, neither too fat nor too thin. Care must be taken that she is not verminous. Both she and the stud must be free from all infections and wormed and their vaccinations must be up to date. The owner of the stud dog is quite within his rights to refuse a mating to a bitch not up to standard. It must be remembered that a valuable show dog at stud could be completely ruined by an infected bitch and such infections could completely decimate the stud dog owner's breeding stock. It is therefore understandable that the stud owner should be wary and execute his right to refuse a stud to a careless bitch owner.

With Long-haired varieties it is usual and desirable to trim the hair from around the vulva, rump and upper parts of the hind legs. A profusion of hair in these parts can hinder a mating and it is also more hygienic at the whelping stage if the hair is removed. The bitch will be out of the show ring for four or five months, giving adequate time for the hair to grow back. However, the stud dog owner should not do this without permission if the bitch owner is not present.

It is not practical to allow dog and bitch to run free in the garden to allow nature to take its course: it is desirable that the mating be carried out under supervision. However, it is not advisable to have more than two persons present at the mating and, ideally but not always possible, both should be known and trusted by dog and bitch. Both dogs can be put off by too many people fussing about them. Conversation should be kept to a minimum, soothing the dogs should take priority. Sudden noises at the crucial time of penetration are frustrating to both dogs and breeders. Radio and televisions should be switched off. Telephones should be unplugged and mobile phones should be tossed out the window. Doors should be locked and all other dogs either taken for a walk or kept as far away as possible.

Do not disturb – honeymoon in progress...

The reluctant bride

A cautionary tale by Pam Evans (Amberliegh)

This is a true Amberliegh story of yesteryear, when Dachshunds of different coats could be mated together.

Heather Bell arrived for her nuptials in fine fettle and great cheer. She admired the garden, seemed delighted with her welcome and smiled in an approving way.

Eventually, after a fruitless weekend, I had to tell her fond owners that Madame was still *intacta*. Nothing had worked. I had offered her three eager boys – she scorned the lot. The last one, Debonair of Daxhead, 3.8kg of pure sex, gave up, yawned and went to sit in the fireplace with his back turned sternly upon Eve, who had tempted – then removed the apple.

I reviewed the situation and decided that all the stops had been pulled out, tried and failed. One faint chance remained. I explained to the owners that, unhopeful as I was, for a last ditch attempt we could try a friend's Miniature Long-haired dog. They answered, 'Please don't trouble; you've had a tiresome weekend.' I sighingly agreed, but wanted to leave no stone unturned.

I ventured forth and arrived at the esteemed fortress of Fettes College, exhausted and extremely disgruntled. I disgorged Miss Bell, who yawned hugely and followed at snail's pace. The door opened. Johnny Bear of Beltrim appeared and, with a piercing shriek of delight, she threw herself with abandon into his arms.

Nine weeks later, almost to the minute, three Smooth puppies of promise made their debut. Sometimes in this world, justice is sadly lacking.

Whelping

I strongly recommend that any problems at or during the whelping of the bitch should be referred immediately to a veterinary surgeon. The following advice is intended for natural and straightforward whelping. I hope to give you a few early warning signs, thus saving your bitch a great deal of distress. To avoid unnecessary suffering, the bitch should be

A Standard Smooth ready to whelp.

95

watched very closely when the time comes. Then you would do well to telephone your vet, asking him or her to stand by in case help is needed.

The bitch should be examined by the vet about a week before she is due to have her puppies to make sure that she is fit, healthy and capable of having her puppies naturally. This may save a lot of distress all round if the vet considers that a cesarean section is probable.

Generally speaking, no two bitches whelp in quite the same way; neither do they behave in exactly the same way when starting to whelp. The gestation period is usually 63 days from the date of the service, but here again, three days before or three days after is not uncommon. A bitch who exceeds her date by three days should be re-examined by the vet to make sure that all is well, that the puppies are alive, and that there are no underlying causes for her lateness.

The whelping box

At least a week before the expected date she should be introduced to her whelping box. This must be a box of adequate size, at least twice her length and twice her width, with a small ledge or straps of wood firmly fixed to the sides at least 8cm from the floor of the box. These reduce the risk of the bitch inadvertently smothering her puppies by rolling on them.

At no time should the bitch be left alone at this critical stage. It may be considered naughty by some, but the author places the whelping box in her bedroom at night, bringing it down into the living area by day. Bitch and author sleep with one eye open for the tell-tale signs, with a low wattage light bulb on all night. (It is not essential, but the author is a self-confessed worry-guts!)

Signs of imminent whelping

The main biological sign that whelping is imminent is a drop in the bitch's temperature. The normal temperature of a dog is 38.6°C (101.5°F). The temperature is taken by inserting the thermometer into the bitch's rectum and holding it steady for about a minute.

Other indications, both physical and behavioural, can be any or all of the following:

- She may become hyperactive, appearing agitated and going from room to room in the house, settling nowhere.
- She may settle down very quietly, stretching out in her box with her head between her paws.
- Most dogs at this stage start scratching up their bedding, and may do this quite frenetically.

   (These are indications that she wants privacy. Turn down the radio or television and ask any visitors to leave. Dim the room and find her a quiet corner where you can observe her without invading her space. What she does not need is an anxious owner and family or children hovering over her.)

- She starts breathing heavily, panting, giving small sharp cries. A soothing voice and encouragement can help at this stage.
- She may continually lick her vulva.
- Most bitches go off their food and may even vomit. This is not a cause for alarm. What you should not do is to try to feed her an extra meal to keep her strength up. She will not be able to deal comfortably with the whelping on a full stomach. Neither can she cope with the placentas she will need to consume. In all probability she would not take an extra meal. If she needed it, then she wouldn't have thrown up in the first place. Always have a fresh bowl of clean, cold water beside the box and continually replace it with fresh, even if she hasn't touched it.
- The vulva becomes swollen and there is a clear mucous discharge. This is normal and nothing to be worried about. The bitch will continually lick herself clean. If the discharge is dark and smells really bad, this could be a bad sign. It may indicate an infection or a dead puppy. Immediate help should be sought.
- A clear sign of true labour is when she starts pushing down, standing four square on all legs or pressing her rear end against the box making straining motions. She may prefer to lie down; she will choose whatever is more comfortable for her.

The most important sign is the straining, and this is when you should make a careful note of the time. If no puppy is produced within two to three hours and she is straining hard you should consider calling the vet for advice.

The birth

As soon as she produces the first puppy you should start timing the interval between each birth, keeping a careful log throughout the whelping. A useful guide might be to expect anything from 10 minutes to an hour and a half between puppies. Here again a careful watch on the bitch should give you some indication whether everything is going well. Continual heaving and straining for a unreasonable length of time is not desirable. It exhausts the bitch and is a sure sign that she may need assistance. Equally, a bitch who suddenly appears to lose all interest, stops straining and settles down to sleep, apparently without labour pains, may be suffering some kind of inertia. The muscles have stopped contracting and are not doing the work of expelling the whelps. An injection from the vet will soon get her going again, but she should be watched carefully. Conversely, heavy straining with no results may mean there is a particularly large puppy blocking the birth channel, or even a dead puppy.

It is useful to have a small bowl of hot water with a few drops of Dettol handy. Several clean towels, cotton wool and round-tipped scissors. Also a good supply of clean bedding, a hot water bottle and a smaller cardboard box. In the case of an exhausted bitch, or a whelp in distress, it may become necessary to use the smaller box with a hot water bottle below the blanket. If, however, extra heat is needed for wet and cold puppies, then it is safer to raise the temperature in the room. The room in any case should be heated to at least 73–76°F. On the other hand, should you have a dead whelp, as soon as the bitch becomes preoccupied with the delivery of her next puppy, the dead whelp should be removed as discreetly as possible and placed well out of her sight and smell.

The first indication that a birth is imminent may be what appears to be a black or dark green balloon-like object the size of a golf ball protruding from the vulva. This is often a cause for panic in the novice. Avoiding technical references, we will call it the water-bag, or sac. This sac is made up of a greenish to black liquid in a membrane skin, and varies in size with how long it takes the bitch to pass it.

The sac is a form of shock absorber, protecting the puppy from injury while it is inside the womb. It also has the function of holding the amniotic fluid. The contractions of the bitch compress this fluid into a balloon shape which emerges first. No attempt should be made to break this sac; in fact the bitch may well do this for herself by constant licking or nipping it with her teeth. After the sac emerges and bursts, the next contraction or two should bring forth the puppy. While this process is happening it is a good idea to wash and soap your hands in the Dettol water in case you need to assist the bitch, although,with a normal whelping, ideally, the bitch will attend to each new offspring herself. The puppy will emerge encased in a membrane, and the bitch's natural instinct will be to tear it away from the whelp, enabling the puppy to breath air for the first time. Then she will sever the umbilical cord attached to the placenta with her teeth. The placenta should follow soon after the birth of the puppy and the bitch will then eat it. This is perfectly natural and it will provide her with protein and nourishment for the first 48 hours.

The puppy will squeak and the bitch will lick it dry; often appearing to push it about in what might seem a rough manner. Actually, she is stimulating the puppy, cleaning, warming and encouraging it to breath; and in no time at all the new arrival will be nosing its way to a nipple to feed.

If all does not go according to plan, and the bitch is somewhat slow in freeing the puppy's muzzle, you may need to break the membrane yourself to enable the puppy to breath. No time should be lost when making up your mind whether to intervene although, strictly speaking, the less intervention the better. The bitch must be given every chance and opportunity to do her own work. You must help only if she shows signs of disinterest. An inexperienced bitch may concentrate too long on the wrong end of the puppy or on cleaning her own vulva and eating the placenta. Bear in mind that lack of oxygen in the post-uterine state (those vital minutes between being dependent on the bitch and being born) may result in brain damage or even death.

Once the nose is free, give the bitch the chance to complete the operation herself. If she does not, you must break the umbilical cord, which will still be attached to the placenta. With finger and thumb, sever it 2–3cm from the puppy's tummy. Great care must be taken not to pull or tug the puppy, as this could cause a hernia. With the puppy well supported, either cut the cord with the round-tipped scissors or nip it with finger and thumb, using a tearing motion.

This is usually all that is needed. The bitch should then be encouraged to take over. She will start licking the puppy and eating the placenta. If she does not, the puppy should be held firmly in a towel and, with a rubbing motion, you should start the process of stimulation by rubbing its sides and tummy, clearing the airways and swabbing the eyes clean. When the puppy starts squeaking and protesting, encourage it to take a nipple.

On rare occasions, more often with a maiden bitch, the bitch may show signs of rejecting the puppy. This may be demonstrated by a rough nosing away of the puppy, pushing it out in the cold, or even growling at it. If so, continue to rub the puppy, making sure it doesn't get cold. When the next puppy is born, before the bitch has time to eat the placenta, gently rub the rejected puppy with it, replacing the smell, and put the puppy in beside the newcomer. In most cases the bitch will start licking both puppies: a sure indication that they have been accepted.

It is a good idea to weight each puppy as it arrives, while still wet, before it starts sucking. Puppies that are obviously small should be examined carefully for imperfections.

When the bitch at last settles down and you think the last puppy has been born, offer the gallant mother something to drink. A little warm milk with added glucose may be offered, but don't be surprised if she ignores it and opts for cool water. She may also be taken outside to relieve herself.

Next, the bitch usually settles down to nurse her young and sleep. She should not be disturbed, especially by visitors. A careful but distant watch should be maintained; late puppies have been known to put in an appearance, confounding everyone, including the vet.

Throughout a normal whelping the owner should merely sit beside the bitch, giving her encouragement in a gentle tone. Assistance should be given only when obvious problems occur. It should be remembered that too much fuss will be transferred to the bitch and she will react to it.

When you feel that the birth is completed, it would be a good idea to ask your vet to examine the dam and her litter. He (or she) will satisfy himself that all the afterbirths are away, perhaps giving the dam an antibiotic in case of latent infections. This antibiotic will be transferred to the puppies through her milk. The vet will also check that the bitch has a milk supply and may give her a further injection to help bring down the milk. Should there be any smaller puppies, or puppies that show signs of being 'bad doers', he will also examine them.

It is better to decide relatively early what to do about badly deformed or weak puppies. Do be advised by your vet. Nothing is sadder or more distressing than losing a puppy days, or sometimes weeks, after its birth. Kindness can sometimes be misguided, and there are numerous stories of owners who have desperately tried to keep a puppy alive with intensive care and 24-hour hand-feeding. Of course there are successes, and these puppies are a delight. But on the whole, nature is a wonderful lady, knowing all too well which puppies can or cannot cope, so do be guided by expert opinion.

A Victorian Whelping

A cautionary tale by Pam Evans (Amberliegh)

This is a true story about a rather affected young lady who regretted an earlier lapse and became a Mama.

Her labour, faint and delicate, commenced at 6.00 pm one evening and, at 7.00 pm on the dot, after one half-hearted heave and with no difficulty whatsoever, out popped puppy number one.

Mama took one quick, despairing look, firmly turned her head to the wall and decided there and then to become an ostrich. 'If I don't look, perhaps it'll disappear,' said the expression on her face.

Not once, in a whelping which could be likened to egg-laying, did she favour her offspring with so much as a glance, until all four sleek seals were lying in a neat row, imbibing satisfactorily. Then, with a sad look, realising that no nanny had been engaged, she took over – and proved to be a model mother.

Postnatal care

For the first three weeks at least, most of the postnatal care needs to be concentrated on the dam. Every assistance should be given to protect her from well meaning and inquisitive human beings. Not only will they upset her, but they will also be the most likely source of any infection brought into the nursery, particularly if they have dogs of their own.

Ambient temperature

Heat must be your number one priority. The nursery area must be at a constant 23–24°C (73–76°F) for the first two weeks at least, perhaps a little less for the Long-haired and Wire-haired varieties. The old Scottish saying that heat is as good as meat is not far wrong. Puppies that have to expend energy generating warmth do not gain the right amount of weight; they are thin and susceptible to illness. The nursery area should be well ventilated but free from draughts. The dam supplies a certain amount of body heat, but keeping the puppies warm can be yet another source of anxiety for her, and distress of any kind can affect the quality and supply of her milk. At this stage she will feed, clean and stimulate her puppies; in fact, she will take care of nearly all their needs.

Feeding

The dam will not need heavy feeding for the first two or three days, and it is not unusual for her to vomit soon after giving birth. Taking into account the amount of protein she has consumed with the placentas, her stomach may be over-burdened. She may also have a loose bowel movement, and this will be dark green, almost black in colour, because of the placentas she has consumed. By both methods, vomiting and diarrhoea, she will be ridding her body of any excess. There is little more you can do apart from cleaning and observing her closely and making sure she has fresh supplies of cool, clean water.

A Standard Smooth two weeks into milk.

Within a couple of days her appetite should return to normal. When it does you must feed her small amounts of nourishing foods such as fish, chicken, rabbit and fresh raw mince, mixed with a little wholemeal mixer. The best mixer I have found, included in all my dogs' diets, is a sliced wholemeal loaf of bread, laid out on a baking tray and dried out in a very low oven.

It is important at this time not to feed your dam entirely on sops, taking particular care of her teeth. She should be encouraged to chew. Her teeth should also be cleaned at least twice weekly, with either a solution of bicarbonate of soda and salt or a good proprietary canine tooth paste. It is not unusual for a dam to have smelly breath after whelping. After all, she uses her mouth to clean the puppies and, while stimulating them, she ingests their urine and bowel motions.

The dam may appear to be thin and in poor condition for a couple of days but this will soon right itself in an otherwise-healthy bitch. After two days she should look nicely covered. The sagging of her 'milk-bar' is natural and to be expected, especially if she is feeding a large litter, but it should not drag down the covering fat and muscle from her top line and she should not appear bony.

It is to be hoped that the owner carried out the proper worming regime before the bitch conceived and at least once mid-pregnancy. If so, and she still looks dreadfully out of condition after the puppies are born, her diet should be adjusted. The puppies are only as good as the feeding they get from the mother. Puppies take whatever they need from the dam, whether her body can afford it or not, but there are limits. They cannot have what she does not have to give. It is not enough to fill her with bulk: she needs good wholesome and nourishing food.

Stimulating the puppies

It is important to check that the dam is cleaning and stimulating the puppy. A very young puppy has little control over its bowel and needs this stimulation to evacuate. Without stimulation the emptying of the rectum is delayed and there is increasing reabsorption of water from its content, so the stools become excessively hard and dry. There have been cases among hand-reared puppies where the owner has neglected this aspect, with the result that the puppies have died from what is essentially a stoppage of the bowels. It is vital to stimulate hand-reared puppies. Using a warm damp flannel you should attempt to imitate the licking motion of the dam. After each feed you should massage and stimulate the abdomen to keep the bowels and bladder moving.

Dew claws

The dam will not want to leave her puppies, but she should be taken out to relieve herself several times a day. These periods should be lengthened as she becomes more confident. When she is out of the way is a good time to inspect the litter.

The vet may have attended to the dew claws when he examined the dam and her litter immediately after the birth. If not, do so within the first two days.

Dachshunds are allowed dew claws on the front feet, but they are undesirable on the back. Few Dachshunds are born with dew claws these days, but if present they should be removed. This is a two-person job. Holding the whelp gently but firmly, place the blunt-tipped scissors close against the skin and neatly sever the dew claws. You will feel the small node. Do not leave any part of the dew claw. There should be little or no bleeding, but if there is a slight seepage you should apply pressure to the point with a piece of lint until it is completely dry. You can also use a light dab of styptic pencil. If you have any doubts about carrying out this operation, ask your vet to do it.

Time is of the essence here. You may not do this on an older whelp. If it has not been done within the first two days you will have to wait until the puppy is at least six months old, and this will involve the use of an anaesthetic.

Daily grooming and hygiene

The daily care of the bitch should include grooming. Her coat should be lightly rubbed over with a damp flannel, and she should be gently brushed to remove all dead hair. This applies to all coats, particularly Long-hairs and Wires.

The daily grooming of the bitch should include her vulva and anal areas. These should be swabbed with cotton wool and warm water with a little mild antiseptic. The blankets should be changed regularly and washed immediately with a few drops of Dettol in the final rinsing water. The blankets should be dried outside whenever possible and should be completely aired before being used again.

Care of the teats

In the general supervision of the dam, care must be taken of her teats. An alert eye must be kept for any inflammation, hard lumps or pain. What you must watch for is mastitis or any sign of an abscess.

Mastitis means inflammation of the breast, and its symptoms appear quite often in the lactating bitch. In one type of mastitis the bitch may have a raised temperature and congested, painful teats. In this case, no pus is produced and the inflammation is hormonal rather than infective in origin. By contrast, in acute suppurative mastitis the teats become infected with Staphylococcus aureus, or less commonly Staphylococcus pyogenes. The bacteria gain access to the teats either via the ducts or through a crack in the nipple. If appropriate antibiotic treatment is not instigated, an abscess may form, resulting in considerable pain and possibly scarring.

It is not uncommon at some time, usually within the first week of feeding, for mammary glands to become engorged and painful. Usually this is caused a build-up of milk due to the whelps preferring the teats that flow more easily. The remedy can be to latch the puppies onto these teats first, effectively taking off the pressure of the milk. Failing this, and if the milk in the teat has become slightly acid, you will have to take the dam aside. Gently bathe her teats with hot (not scalding) water and express some of the milk until the teats become softer and more manageable for the whelps. Failure and neglect to do this could result in blood poisoning, which in extreme cases could prove fatal.

Weaning
Early weaning should be considered only if it is obvious that the puppies are not satisfied or progressing. With large litters is may be as early as two-and-a-half weeks. Smaller litters

The start of weaning: a three-week-old Miniature Smooth litter
learning to eat from a bowl.

Two Miniature Smooth litters together at the 'dining table'.

A four-week-old Standard Smooth puppy.

may be perfectly satisfied on the dam's milk for three to three-and-a-half weeks. Mother's milk is best, but if the whelps are restless between feeds you must consider whether or not they are satisfied.

Weaning should be introduced slowly. Ready Brek or baby rusks are good to start with. Mix the cereal into a thin gruel with milk heated to blood heat and fill a saucer. Take each puppy individually and gently touch the mouth with the liquid. Some get the idea quickly and lap quite greedily while others may need a little patient coaching. When the puppy is lapping well, do support the chest and neck, for the first few times at least. To begin with, morning and last thing at night is usually enough to be going on with, but it depends on how much milk the dam has. These meals can be increased gradually and the menu can then be varied as new tastes are introduced. Such things as raw, double-minced meat and scrambled egg should be included at least twice or three times a week. In one of the meals a multiple vitamin with added trace elements, something like SA37 or Stress, which contains calcium (good for bone development), can be added according to the manufacturers' instructions. However, these additives are not strictly necessary for a puppy who is already getting a varied and nourishing diet, and some proprietary brands, such as Ready Brek and Farley's rusks, already have added vitamins. The same can be said of all brands of dried baby milk, sometimes used instead of cow's milk. Common sense must prevail when deciding if your dam and puppies actually need supplementary additives. One of the best milks to use is goat's milk, if you can get it.

As the puppies get older and more independent, the bitch will increase her time away from them, sometimes appearing to be inattentive. She may also show signs of becoming cross at feeding times and, if this should happen, you would be well advised to examine the puppies' nails. All puppies when feeding tend to knead the 'milk bar' and can scratch the dam's teats quite cruelly. All puppies' nails grow rapidly, becoming like sharp needles, but it is a simple operation to nip off the hooked ends carefully with a small pair of scissors.

Independence
By the time the puppies are enjoying four meals a day, the bitch should be encouraged to spend more time away from the litter throughout the day. She will decide when her teats are becoming uncomfortably

Seven-week-old Standard Smooth puppies with their dam. Note that, although they are weaned, they still like a drink from Mum!

Bonnerhill de A-Nis at eight weeks.

Bonnerhill de A-Nis at five months.

engorged with milk and return to her brood to have the puppies suckle off the excess. Her time away from the puppies should be extended gradually until she is only sleeping with them at night.

Long before this you will discover that the bitch is less inclined to clean up completely after the whelps. After all, they are now producing waste products which she has not produced with her own milk. The stools will no longer be yellow in colour and the urine is much stronger.

At this time the puppies should be transferred to an area where the bed is

Bonnerhill Esprit d'Amour at eight weeks.

Bonnerhill Esprit d'Amour at five months.

separated by a play area. If forced to do so, the whelps have no option but to wet their blankets, but few puppies wet their bedding if presented with an alternative. They will move out instinctively to urinate in a corner of the run, using newspaper or sawdust. This is an excellent way to encourage a puppy to use newspaper, a practice you may well find useful later, when real training begins.

Worming

All puppies, along with the dam, should have an initial worming programme. They should be wormed at three weeks, five weeks and seven weeks. It is not always easy to find which puppy has been sick after a worming, so I rarely use tablets or the cheaper brands of worming preparations bought over the counter in pet shops. My personal preference is for something like Strongid. This is a paste in a tube, much like toothpaste in appearance. It is palatable, easy to measure out and can be given at any time without a starving. It does not scour the puppies and they are rarely sick. It is only available from a vet. As with all medicines and potions, do seek professional advice.

If you don't have the time, don't have the puppies!

Socialisation

Throughout the developing stages of your puppies life, please don't forget the personal touch. Once they start feeding independently from the dam they should be handled and played with. There should be plenty of toys to create an interest and a time set aside for personal contact. There is nothing quite so sad as segregated puppies, sad little faces that can only gaze longingly through wire fencing. If you don't have the time, then don't have the puppies!

8 In sickness and in health

With dogs and humans alike, there comes a time when illness and disease seem to strike from nowhere. In many cases these tragedies can be avoided with sensible care and forethought. There are some instances when, although every precaution has been taken, the most careful among us may be hit by an infection. For instance, sometimes Dachshunds,

Dachshunds are alert, active hounds. They are not lap dogs.

especially those who travel to dog shows, may come into contact with other dogs whose owners are not quite so caring. However, illness, disease and accidents are often preventable.

You and your vet

In all things relating to your dog's welfare, you must be guided by an expert opinion. The saying *a little knowledge is a dangerous thing* certainly applies: old wives tales and secret recipes are gambles that should not be weighed against the cost of the vet's fee. There has been a measure of bad press relating to the diverse differences in veterinary fees. it is true that they differ, so do shop around for a decent veterinary clinic or surgery or take out insurance. Do be up-front about what you can afford; most vets are understanding and allow large bills to be paid off in instalments. There are also free clinics, although, if you have paid a high price for your dog, perhaps you should have considered the cost of its care before buying it. The dog's welfare must be considered. Small dogs can cost as much as £700 a year to keep. In the case of show exhibits, the cost of entry fees and travelling far outweighs the normal yearly veterinary fees for a healthy dog.

We've all had bad experiences of one kind or another. I had a vet whose mouth was shaped for a 'tenner'. From nail clipping to worming tablets, everything was £10 or multiples thereof. I am happy to say that I now have a clinic which employs half a dozen vets, whose expertise is far ranging, and every bill I receive is itemised down to the individual cost of a single tablet.

Do not be influenced by the fact that you've known a certain vet for years if he's a kindly old codger, not exactly up to all these modern ideas. The quality of your vet can be the difference between life and death for your dog.

Preventive vaccinations

One major precaution is to have your dog inoculated as a puppy. It must have its first inoculations between eight and twelve weeks old. In this you must be guided by your veterinary surgeon, and you will probably find that each vet recommends a different age.

Perhaps we should consider the reasons for this. We know that different areas have different risks. For instance, the urban Dachshund may not come into contact with many farm animals; on the other hand, those residing in rural or greenbelt areas probably will. Your vet will be aware of any contagious or infectious diseases in his or her area and may well advise precautionary measures.

Dachshunds love company – both canine and human.

Articles sometimes appear in the canine newspapers and magazines advocating the substitution of herbal preventive remedies and curative medicines. I reserve judgment about this. Quite simply, I don't know enough to pass an opinion. While several herbal remedies such as garlic and seaweed extract are beneficial, and many modern medicines derive from nature's larder, until I have irrefutable evidence that these remedies are capable of replacing those first vital inoculations I must stay with what I know to be effective. For lesser matters, many of us indulge in both alternative and orthodox medicine, but not to the extent of putting our dogs at risk. Your dog relies on you for more than just friendship – it trusts you with its life. It is unfair to subject your dog to experimental uses of unproven medicines when it is ill. Prevention is better than cure, so having your dog vaccinated must be a priority.

What are vaccinations, and what do we get?

Firstly, you will be given a record card listing all vaccinations the dog has received with dates, and this should be kept in a safe place for referral. It will list all primary and booster injections.

Initially your puppy should be vaccinated against: distemper, hepatitis, leptospirosis, parvovirus and parainfluenza. These injections are of multiple ingredients, which means just two or, sometimes three, first injections. Dogs who are likely to come into contact with other dogs (for instance, at shows or in boarding kennels) should also be protected against kennel cough. This is a simple procedure: a few drops of something like Intrac are administered into the respiratory system through the nose, as nose drops.

The horrifying diseases are described in more detail below. Of them, distemper and parvovirus are the most dangerous. It is also necessary to protect against hepatitis and the two leptospiral diseases. Some hepatitis vaccines also protect against an infectious agent implicated in the kennel cough syndrome.

Whilst no guarantee can be given, the chances of your dog contracting these diseases after being injected are slim, and you can take comfort in the knowledge that, should they

Elizabeth Fulton's children with Wires. If there is mutual respect, dogs and children can have great relationships.

succumb, the degree of seriousness will be lessened and your dog will have a fighting chance. Without being vaccinated, your dog runs a very high risk of contracting one of them.

Distemper

This is a virus infection, usually complicated by a secondary bacterial invasion. The first major signs are a cough, followed by a high temperature, lethargy, loss of appetite, red eyes, runny nose and noisy breathing, with possible diarrhoea. Subsequently, usually after a few weeks, there are the nervous signs: a nervous twitch, fits or paralysis may develop.

These symptoms are often followed by a thickening of the pads and the nose (*hyperkeratosis*), which is why the disease is sometimes called *hardpad*.

The wonderful gloss on Aust Ch Hannalex Black Heidi's coat
bears witness to her excellent state of health.

Infectious canine hepatitis

(Also known as *Rubarth's Disease* or *Viral Hepatitis*).

This highly contagious disease is caused by canine adenovirus and has no connection with hepatitis in man. Puppies up to a year old are most commonly affected, although dogs of all ages are susceptible. The early and major signs are a lack of appetite and general illness with pale gums and conjunctivitae. Raised temperature, vomiting, and diarrhoea may then develop, with abdominal pain. Jaundice (yellowing) of the whites of the eyes may occur.

Leptospirosis

This is a disease caused by a group of bacteria called *Leptospires*, and dogs can be infected by two of these: *Leptospira icterohaemorrhagiae* and *Leptospira canicola*. Both can be passed on to humans.

Leptospira icterohaemorrhagia: Symptoms are a high temperature, severe thirst, frequency of urination, abdominal pain, depression, possibly ulceration of the mouth, a coated tongue, diarrhoea containing blood, jaundice and persistent vomiting. The most important prevention is initial vaccination and annual boosters. In addition, any contact with rats or rat infested water must be avoided and, in suspect areas, food and drinking bowls should not be left outdoors overnight.

Leptospira canicola: The signs are similar to those described under Leptospira icterohaemorrhagiae except that jaundice is seen much less frequently, or is less marked. Mild cases with few signs occur quite frequently, but this infection can damage the kidneys and this condition may become critical later in life. Again, vaccination is the surest

Glamorous Long-hairs require rather more coat care than Smooths do.

prevention. Most dogs who recover excrete bacteria in their urine for anything up to a year – a matter to consider if you are wondering whether to keep young puppies on the same premises. However, prompt vaccination of puppies at eight to twelve weeks is advocated, and regular annual boosters are vital.

Parvovirus

This is a small, persistent and very hardy virus. Two forms of canine parvovirus are recognised.

Canine parvovirus myocarditis: This form of parvovirus is now becoming rare as most breeding bitches will have some antibody to the infection, either through previous exposure to the disease or through vaccination.

Intestinal canine parvovirus: This is the most common form of parvovirus. It affects dogs from four weeks of age right into old age, but most severely in their first year, when the disease can be rapid and fatal. The signs in this form of the disease are depression, severe and protracted vomiting, abdominal pain, refusal of food and water, and very profuse diarrhoea, often with a considerable blood content.

Parvovirus is usually rapid in resolution: if the dog is to survive it will be noticeably better within four to five days of the start of the symptoms. Yet again, early vaccination and yearly boosters are the surest means of prevention. Be warned: when parvovirus is suspected, not only should the dog be kept in isolation from other dogs but all members of the household should avoid contact with other dogs, because the virus can be carried on clothing and shoes. This disease takes a heavy toll on young puppies and elderly dogs.

Parasites

Worms

There are two main types of parasitic worm: roundworm *(Toxocara canis)* and tapeworm *(Dipylidium caninum)*.

All puppies are born with roundworm, having been infected in the womb. Although infection becomes less common in older dogs, a regular worming programme is still extremely important. In rare instances accidental human infection can occur, which may cause eye or other problems, particularly in young children. Worms are only seen if your dog vomits, rarely in faeces. However, large numbers of eggs are produced in the gut and these are passed out in the dog's faeces and can become a danger to public health.

Treatment is simple and relatively distress-free for dogs these days. All puppies, (along with their dam) should be wormed at three weeks, five weeks, seven weeks and thereafter at monthly intervals until the age of six months. Subsequently, regular worming should be carried out at four to six monthly intervals.

Tapeworms can be very long and consist of small segments all joined together to form the 'tape'. The most common tapeworm *(Dipylidium caninum)* spends part of its life cycle in the flea, but your dog can become infected with other types of tapeworm by eating uncooked and infected meat and offal. Tapeworms shed their segments constantly, and these are sometimes seen as white particles in your dog's faeces or around the anus. Not only do they look unpleasant; they also cause irritation.

All combination worming remedies are very effective. Large numbers of worms can affect your dog's health seriously, particularly in the case of young puppies, where a heavy infestation can cause loss of weight, sickness or even complete blockage of the gut.

Most worming products these days are effective combination wormers, so there is no need to identify the species. Your vet will advise.

Jack enjoys a romp with his new owner
in quarantine in Australia.

Fleas

Fleas are no respecters of pedigree and, unfortunately, they are agile, disease-carrying little beggars. They also infest the house and enjoy biting people.

Numerous products are on the market: shampoos, flea collars, powders, sprays and those that need to be administered orally. Because of the long cocoon stage of the developing flea it is important to set up a programme in which the treatment is repeated at regular intervals. All carpets and upholstery must be vacuumed, pet bedding washed and a household spray used. This will help destroy the adult flea and the immature fleas as they hatch.

Mites, lice and ticks

The same measures can be taken against other parasitic infestations such as microscopic mite, sucking lice, biting lice and ticks.

Mange

Mange is a parasitic skin disease, and the most common form is Sarcoptic Mange. The symptoms are scratching and small red pustules. If neglected, the skin will become bare and rough-looking in patches, and these will soon spread to the whole body.

Because this condition is caused by a mite too small to be seen with the naked eye, laboratory diagnosis is crucial. Your vet will prescribe the proper treatment, which will include a specially medicated shampoo and an ointment. If your dogs are housed in outside kennels, all bedding must be burnt and the kennel fumigated to rid it of these disease-carrying mites. All hair from the dog must be vacuumed up and the dust bag in your machine burnt. Rely heavily on your vet's advice and practice strict hygiene. Home remedies may be effective but will take longer to work, resulting in more distress to the dog and greater risk to humans. Modern medication is quicker and more effective.

Other skin problems

Ringworm

This is a contagious disease (brought about by contact: touching) as opposed to infectious (communicated to the environment through the air). The problem presents itself as bare, circular patches, varying in size. The underlying skin looks dry and rough with small red blemishes.

The dog must be strictly segregated from other animals and the affected areas treated daily. There are plenty of old remedies for this disease, but do consult your vet: modern remedies are more effective than the Tincture of Iodine and Mercury ointments once used. This disease is contagious to humans and other dogs, so strict hygiene must be practised.

Eczema

Eczema is not contagious or infectious. It is an inflammatory condition of the skin. As in humans, this condition tends to flare up at moments of stress. Much can be done to ease the irritation. There may be times when the condition seems to clear, only to re-appear again. Your vet will recommend suitable treatment and possibly advise about improving the general condition of your dog.

Conditions affecting bitches

Eclampsia
This is a very serious and worrying condition in nursing bitches and it warrants urgent and immediate treatment. It is caused by a calcium deficiency. The bitch appears drowsy and unsteady on her legs. There may be a twitching of the muscles, followed by convulsions. She will need immediate injections of calcium, and the future care of the litter should be discussed with the vet. It may well mean hand-rearing.

Metritis
The symptom is an abnormal discharge from the uterus after whelping. This may be caused by the retention of a dead puppy or an afterbirth (placenta), or by an infection. Veterinary treatment must be given.

Pyometra
In this condition, most common in middle-aged bitches, pus forms in the uterus. The bitch will be markedly unwell; she will vomit and be thirsty and listless. There may also be a putrid-smelling discharge. This condition needs immediate veterinary treatment if it is not to prove fatal.

> **Warning about hygiene:** Breeders who use petroleum jelly (Vaseline) to ease penetration when a small or maiden bitch is being serviced should practise strict hygiene at all times. Petroleum jelly, like cooking fat and oil, holds a certain amount of heat and rarely drops its temperature. It is therefore an ideal culture material for bacteria. It is all too easy to transfer infection in this way. Always take the petroleum jelly from the jar with a sterile spatula and reseal the lid immediately. Scrub the hands before inserting the finger into the bitch's vaginal area. Better still, use surgical gloves.

Miscellaneous

Anal glands
These small scent glands are situated under the skin at each side of the anus. When they fail to empty they may need to be expressed: a simple, if unpleasant, procedure. The dog often appears to scrape its bottom along the grass or carpet and may attempt to bite the area. This may also be a symptom of worm infestation.

Bath the area with a dilute solution of warm water and Dettol. Then, using two dampened pads of cotton-wool, empty the glands by expressing them gently. Keep the area clean and disinfected.

Dachshunds come in various shapes, sizes and colours.

Choking

The most common causes of choking are foreign objects too large to pass down the gullet. Stones, pieces of stick, and even bones can become fixed at the back of the throat. The object may be removed with the fingers or long forceps. The obstruction should be removed speedily to avoid asphyxia. You must remain calm to avoid distressing the animal further, and it is helpful to have a second handler to hold the dog steady.

If all attempts fail to remove the object, an effort must be made to force it downwards, allowing the dog to breath. If this is successful the dog should be taken to the vet, who must ascertain that the object has not become wedged in the lower oesophagus. The vet will then explore all avenues to make sure the object is not dangerous to the dog. He or she may keep the dog in overnight to make sure there is no blockage.

Enteritis

This is an inflammatory condition of the bowels which can be caused by an allergy or infected food. The symptoms are diarrhoea and sickness. In extreme cases there may be blood in the faeces.

The greatest danger here is dehydration which, if untreated, can prove fatal. This is a another case where you must consult your vet. After which, pay particular attention to the washing of feeding and water bowls.

A personal hint: Soak the bowls with very hot water from the tap and a Milton sterilising tablet as used for babies' bottles. Leave the dishes covered with this solution until the water cools enough for the dishes to be washed in the normal way.

Hernia

A hernia is any protrusion of an internal organ through the wall of the cavity that normally contains it. Most hernias involve the gut, the most common form being the *inguinal hernia*, which causes a lump in the groin. Inguinal hernias should be repaired by surgery, especially in bitches, and the bitch should not be bred from until the hernia is safely repaired. Inguinal hernias sometimes develop in obese dogs with weakened abdominal muscles.

Umbilical hernias are not uncommon in puppies. These may be caused by rough handling by the bitch when detaching the placenta and breaking the umbilical cord. In some cases the hernia diminishes of its own accord as the muscles of the abdomen strengthen.

Poisoning

The symptoms are usually vomiting, abdominal pain, a rigid and unnatural gait, difficulty in breathing and collapse. The dog should be made to vomit by inducing an emetic of warm salt water. The dog should then be kept warm and veterinary attention should be sought immediately.

Aust Chs Quellental Kelele and Tinsnips Gothe Wholehog get into the festive mood.

Seizures

These are sudden convulsions, usually caused by epilepsy, high fever, poisoning or hysteria. The *petit mal* attack, a lesser form of epilepsy, may be a short, quick loss of consciousness that may amount to no more than a momentary silence or loss of attention. The *grand mal*, the typical form of epileptic attack, is when the patient becomes unconscious, falls, shakes and is incontinent. The dog may hurt itself, perhaps biting its tongue during an attack, and it cannot be roused from the attack even by painful stimuli. Afterwards, it recovers consciousness slowly.

There are different variations on this pattern, with epileptic attacks ranging in duration and seriousness.

A dog developing convulsions as the result of a high fever is not necessarily epileptic. Neither should simple fainting should be confused with epilepsy, even if the dog shows minor twitching movements. There are also diseases such as diabetes mellitus which may produce loss of consciousness.

Attacks happening for the first time should always be referred to the vet, who will be grateful for a full and accurate description of the seizure.

Slipped disk (herniated disk)

The intervertebral disks, which act largely as 'shock absorbers' between the vertebral bodies and convey flexibility of the spine, may herniate, or 'slip' forwards or sideways, as a result of trauma. Other causes can be weaknesses of the retaining ligaments or changes occurring in the fibrous consistency of the disk's outer wall. If the disk slips forwards it may impinge on the spinal cord or nerves leading from it, causing pain, weakness and numbness.

X-rays of the spine can show loss of disk space between particular vertebral bodies but not the disk itself; the disk itself is not opaque to X-rays. Injection of a radiopaque dye (a myelogram) is required to define the precise extent of a disk's protrusion forward.

Treatment depends largely on the severity of the symptoms and the nature of the injury. The first treatment is complete rest. If rest is ineffective, the bones of the spine may be stretched by traction. If all else fails, or the symptoms recur, surgical treatment may be necessary to remove the protruded section of the disk.

Stings

It is not rare for a dog to be stung on the face, lips or muzzle. Any sting should be removed and the area gently bathed with an antiseptic lotion. Swelling of the face is usually temporary. However, a wasp or bee sting inside the mouth or on the tongue could be serious. Veterinary assistance should be sought immediately.

9 Show grooming

Smooth-haired Dachshunds

Bathing the Smooth-haired Dachshund in preparation for showing is a matter of trial and error, and it is not a bad idea to have a dry run (no pun intended!)

Bathing

The quality of water in Britain varies; some areas have 'soft' water, some 'hard'. It follows that the way in which various commercial shampoos react with water varies according to area. Hard water can bring about a dull looking coat, with an almost grey sheen, which will not show a black-and-tan Dachshund to its best

Ch/Ir Ch Wingcrest Penny Royal, owned by May Batterson-Webster, demonstrates a lovely gloss on a smooth coat.

advantage. The answer in hard-water areas is either to keep a rain barrel or to experiment with different brands of shampoo. It can also help to add a little vinegar to the final rinsing water, and a very small quantity of baby oil massaged onto the palm and then rubbed across the coat can be helpful. A word of warning: this should be done a day or so before showing, as any substance applied to the coat to enhance the colour and texture or change or alter the dog's natural appearance is strictly forbidden.

It is reasonable then to expect that dogs from different areas need to be bathed at different intervals before showing. You are aiming for a waxy shine and for hair that lies flat and shows off your dog to its best advantage. For some dogs this may indicate a bath the night before the show; for others, three to four days beforehand may be more effective.

Too much bathing strips the natural oils from a dog's coat, which may result in loose flakes of dead skin rising to the surface like dandruff. Here again, baby oil or almond oil massaged into the coat prior to bathing can help.

I am sure that most exhibitors will agree with me when I say that these unsightly flakes always seem to appear 10 minutes before you go into the ring. Be assured that, unless your dog is suffering from some kind of skin disorder, everything will settle down. Should you notice this at the show, a dampened flannel is helpful. Failing that, it is a good idea to carry a small pump spray of water with you – but make sure that the spray contains only water. The Kennel Club is precise, and the penalties are strict.

Trimming

Very little, if any, trimming is necessary for Smooth-haired Dachshunds. You may use round-tipped scissors to trim off the whiskers from the side of the muzzle if you think this will enhance the dog's outline. This is something practised in the United States of America, but not so often in the United Kingdom. The whiskers are clipped close to the skin without touching the surrounding hair on the cheeks and over the eyes. If necessary, you may trim any long or unsightly hairs from the front of the neck and all wispy hairs level with the coat. The same goes for those on the underside of the tail and the feet. These odd hairs are thought to be a throw-back to when it was permitted to breed Long-haired Dachshunds to Smooths - a practice not permitted today.

Immaculately groomed: Aust Ch Rossini Sunset Debutante, owned by Mr and Mrs Bethel.

Teeth

Particular attention should be paid to the mouth, and a show dog's teeth should be cleaned daily.

Nails

Nails should be kept always in trim, and perhaps you should have a regular time each week for tipping and filing them, so that it becomes routine. If a dog's nails have got out of hand and the nails have become too long to cut in one operation, a weekly tipping and daily road-walking routine will soon reduce them.

Hold the dog's paw firmly and, using nail trimmers, cut away from you. Shave a little off the tips weekly. This will cause the small vein in the nail to retreat back into the nail, allowing you to trim the nails to the desired length without causing bleeding. The nail clippers should be sharp; if they tend to split the nail the blade needs changing. If this does not work, ask your vet to trim them the first time, and afterwards abide by the golden rule of attending to your dog's nails weekly.

Ears

As part of the weekly routine, attention should be paid to the ears. A soft cloth moistened with almond oil to clean the inside of the leathers is all that is needed, remembering that the first sign of neglected ears is a rather bad smell. Ears should be sweet-smelling at all times. It is dangerous to dig into any ears with hair clips and cotton wool buds, and we must never dig into the inner ear chamber. Two drops in each ear of an ordinary solution of ear drops, something like Johnston's or Shirley's Ear Drops, is all that is needed. This is an added precaution against grass mites and any other menace your dog might pick up in the garden.

Long-haired Dachshunds

Daniel Roberts (Swanford)

Daniel Roberts shares the Swanford affix with Mrs Margaret Swann, and this compatible partnership works extremely well. They have been friends for many years – in fact, since Daniel was a schoolboy. As a lad Daniel worked weekends with Margaret and her dogs. Later, almost seven years ago now, Margaret had a horrifying accident and, to Daniel's credit, he stepped in and helped care for her dogs while Margaret was in hospital.

Margaret later decided to go into partnership with Daniel and this brought about what has proved to be a most congenial arrangement.

Margaret's pedigree (if you'll forgive the pun) is impeccable, and her knowledge well earned. She came into the breed in 1970. Before that her main interest was the German Shepherd. As a breeder of Standard Long-haired Dachshunds, an exhibitor and all round canine enthusiast, she has much to offer the breed.

Daniel writes:

Those who think that all that is involved in preparing the Long-haired Dachshund for show is a brush and comb and a nice lead are sadly mistaken. If you are a newcomer to the most glamorous of the three varieties, I would suggest that you go along to any major championship show to learn how the Standard or Miniature Long is presented. We are blessed with some very knowledgeable breeders who, once they know you are serious about the breed, will be only too pleased to guide you.

When you have made the decision that this is the breed for you, the first thing I would advice would be to take time over the bathing and grooming of your dog. This should not be done in a hurry.

Between shows the novice should practise for the

Ch Swanford Kamador, beautifully prepared for the ring.
Photo: Diane Pearce

Ch Dandydayo Troublemaker of Swanford ready for action.
Photo: Gibbs

best results to discover which type of coat your dog has. It may be surprising, but there are so many different types of hair structures within the variety. There are coarser-haired types, fine-haired, wavy, dry, even oily coated dogs, and each specimen must be treated as an individual.

By practising between shows you will have time to try different methods of grooming and so adjust your method.

Grooming and very basic ring-class training ideally should start when the puppy is about six weeks. Little and often is the best method for both the dog and owner. At all costs your puppy must not get bored with the procedure, and although it may be frustrating, you must not show any signs if ill-temper. Using a steel comb on the puppy you should gently start combing along the body and ears; at all times praising your dog for being such a clever boy/girl to allow this. Speak in a soothing tone, and treating it as fun at this stage is best. As the dog gets older you may then become a little firmer, working up every day until he starts his ring-training in earnest.

Teeth

As with children, a puppy's mouth is important. It must learn relatively early that its teeth must be inspected on command. Great care should be practised when examining a puppy's mouth; it is a tender area. Dogs go through a teething period at around the age of three to six months. They gradually lose their baby teeth when the permanent adult teeth push the shallow-rooted milk-teeth free from the gums. This relates to all Dachshunds whatever their size or variety. Do remember that rough or heavy handling at this stage could put a dog off having his mouth examined for life.

Adult dogs should not have many problems with tartar if fed on a correct diet. A dry type of biscuit or even the odd knuckle bone will help to keep the teeth tartar-free. For older dogs you may need a descaler to remove the tartar, but great care and gentleness is needed to avoid damaging the gums or causing pain. If in doubt then do rely on the vet to do this. There are plenty of canine dental toothpastes on the market, and toothbrushes especially designed for the dog's mouth.

Feet

Trimming the excess hair and tailoring the feet on the Long-haired Dachshund has always been a pet hate of mine, it always seems to grow back so quickly, and of course the nails must be kept short. This is not so difficult if one starts early with the puppy. From about two weeks plus the nails should be clipped, and by starting so early the 'quicks' in the bed of the nails remain withdrawn and rarely bleed.

The real trimming of a Long-hair need only involve the foot area. Starting on the bottom of the pads the excess hair should be trimmed off the pads. I would add that hair growing between the pads can distort the feet, which should be compact and tight.

Once the pad area has been completed, the front 'top' of the toes and instep will need to be tidied. Following the natural shape of the dog, any long or unsightly hair may be removed with the forefinger and thumb to give the dog an all-over smooth and tidy outline.

Bathing and grooming

Bathing can be the most difficult part of the preparation, but it is most important if you are to give your dog an overall outline and finish. The dog's coat naturally grows at different stages and I have found that the most difficult age to prepare a dog for showing is around the six to ten months, when the coat tends to be very thick and lacks strength. All our dogs are bathed and blow-dried

The last touches are put to an American Long before the show.

with a hand-held dryer before every show, and we would never present a dog which had not been bathed.

Shampoo is another case for trial and error. I always reckon that, if a shampoo is good enough for me, it's good enough for my dog. Most shampoos designed for human beings are more natural and contain far less chemicals. If you remember that the coat must resemble that of the Irish Setter, lying flat and straight, then this will give you something to aim for. We personally find that shampoos containing coconut extract are particularly effective. Again, in the summer when our dogs come into contact with all kinds of garden pests and possibly fleas, Phillips Shampoo is most helpful (taking great care not to get it in the eyes), but at the same time making sure that the face area is well washed. The face is most probably the dirtiest area on a Dachshund; after all, he does use it for practically everything!

Once well-lathered, rinse off and then repeat the process if necessary. You may if you wish use a conditioner, although this should be well rinsed out of the coat. The purpose of the conditioner is more for ensuring a tangle-free coat when brushing and combing it out than for altering the structure of the coat.

Towel dry around the ears and feet. Then, with the hair-dryer on a low setting, start drying the coat. Using the dryer about 20cm from the coat, start by facing in the general direction in which the coat lies. This is a long, slow job, if it's done correctly. Remembering that the coat must lie flat and using a steel comb, both brush and comb the hair dry under the low heat. The whole process takes on average about an hour and a half.

Throughout this procedure you must make sure your dog is standing up, so that no kinks occur. Once the dog is dry, with no damp areas at all, you may place it to rest on a flat surface. We say flat because we do not want any curls or kinks to appear.

I know there are other ways of doing this, but this method has always been my most successful. And while it is tempting to leave the dogs coat a little damp, it is not a good idea.

With a damp coat you run the risk of less shine. I would add all the same that, should it be a really nice warm day, then it is a good idea to take your dog for a quick walk in the sun.

After giving the dog an hour or two's rest, pop it back onto the grooming table and inspect for any kinked areas that might have developed. If they have, damp them lightly with water and re-dry.

If on inspection you notice a few odd hairs on the head sticking up, remove them with the forefinger and thumb method. There are advocates for the removal of whiskers, but this is a matter of personal choice. We do not find that it enhances the head or expression – especially if the dog develops designer-stubble.

And that's basically that, as far as grooming and bathing are concerned. As you can see, we need very little trimming or tailoring, which makes the variety a good choice, particularly if you are not too good at scissor work.

A 'thank you'

I cannot finish without saying that, without the help of Margaret Swann, whose famous Swanford Kennel of Long-hairs has produced the breed record holder Ch Swanford Arrandor, together with over 40 world-wide champions, my time with this wonderful variety would not have been so exciting. For good, honest advice, Margaret Swann must surely be one of the finest and most knowledgeable people in the breed today, and I take this opportunity to thank her. Thank you, Margaret.

Wire-haired Dachshunds
Elizabeth Fulton (Bothlyn)

The best advice I can offer to owners of Wire-haired Dachshunds, Standard or Miniature, is to obtain a really good photograph and study it closely to see exactly what fringes and beards to leave on the dog. Of the three coats, this is by far the hardest to groom because, within the variety, there are several types of coat. We will concentrate on the dog who has grown out: that is to say, has its full coat but is intended for showing in a few weeks' time.

Again, you must start with the basic grooming equipment. You will need small, blunt-nosed scissors, sharp hairdresser's scissors, nail clippers, a natural bristle brush, two metal combs (wide-toothed and fine-toothed), and a set of stripping knives. The stripping knives should not be the kind that uses razor blades; your aim is to pull out the hair, not cut it.

Brushing and combing

Do not bath the dog, as this softens the coat. Instead, start by brushing out the coat thoroughly with the bristle brush. Then, using the combs, thoroughly comb out any tangles on the legs, chest and beard.

Stripping and trimming

The object of stripping is to remove all dead hair with the finger and thumb. To do this, catching a few strands at a time, the hair must be pulled, using elbow rather than wrist action.

Take the hair out as evenly as possible, as too much at a time will take out clumps. As with Long-hairs, this time-consuming activity does not all have to be done in one sitting. Hand stripping gives the best results and should not be done in a hurry.

Head: Always stripping the hair in the direction in which it grows, clean off the top of the head to the undercoat, using your fine stripping knife, leaving the eyebrows and beard. Then, using either the fine stripping knife or your forefinger and thumb, remove the hairs to strip clean the insides of the ears as close to the skin as you can manage. Next, take the hair on the cheeks down as short as possible. The beard should be left from the corner of the mouth forward, and then evened up with the thumb and forefinger or the tip of the fine stripping knife, the blade being steadied by your thumb. Remove the hair

Elizabeth Fulton with Ch Bothlyn Mastercraftsman at Crufts 1994. Photo: Carol Ann Johnson

from between the eyes and the ridge just in front of the eyes. It helps to comb the eyebrows forward, enabling you to get a better view of the final result. Then, starting from the outside corner, pull the hair as close to the eye as possible, gradually working your way toward the inside corners, leaving the hair to graduate longer as you move towards the inside corner of the eye. This should produce a pointed effect to the eyebrow.

Neck: Using the fine stripping knife, start stripping the underside of the neck down to the breastbone, following the contour of the natural 'V' shape. Start at the corner of the mouth and work your way down the breastbone, always mindful to keep to the inside of the natural ridges of the 'V' shape, which is formed by the way the hair naturally grows. Repeat this process on the other side of the dog until you are left with the ridges. Now remove the ridges with the fine stripping knife. Leave the hair below the breastbone, which you will deal with when you come to the furnishings.

Topline: Returning to the top and sides of the neck and the topline of the dog, remove the hair down the back of the neck and on both sides of it, working your way down the back of the dog and both sides, including the belly. All the topcoat should be removed, leaving only the undercoat.

Hindquarters: After removing the body coat, start stripping the tail down to the undercoat. Then, using your double rounded scissors, cut the hair around the testicles (or vulva for a bitch) and anal area. Carefully, with the scissors, strip the hair in the genital and all pink areas, including the ridges on the back of the hips.

Legs: Everything below where the flanks meet the stifle is considered leg furnishings. Make sure all the leg furnishings are well combed out before attempting to tackle them. Comb the hair straight and trim in a straight line, shortening it by about one third its length. Repeat on all four legs. On dogs with extremely harsh coats only the tips of the furnishings need trimming. This trimming should go all the way down to, and including, the feet.

Feet: Tidy each foot by trimming its edges to give a neat appearance. Remove all hair from between the pads of the foot.

Forequarters: Facing the dog, smooth the shoulders and take off all the stray hairs from between the shoulder and breastbone, taking all hair down to the undercoat.

What you are aiming for is a dog that, from a distance, looks almost like a Smooth-haired Dachshund. It is only as you come close that you see the beard and well-defined eyebrows of the Wire.

Stripping a Wire is a complicated procedure that takes a lot of practice. Preparation of showing should be undertaken at least nine weeks prior to the show, depending on the coat. A softer coat takes longer to grow to perfection, while a harder one attains all the necessary characteristics much more quickly.

Ch Bothlyn Blue Print. Photo: David Dalton

To sum up: consider having the initial stripping performed by an expert, especially if you have never owned or exhibited a Wire-haired Dachshund before. I'm sure it is easier to learn from personal observation, so I would urge you to seek expert advice.

Editor's note: As editor and compiler of this book, one over-riding lesson I have learned is the generosity of all Wire-haired owners. The most expert in their field have been very generous with their advice, and all those approached have demonstrated a passion for the furthering of their breed and variety.

Ch Bothlyn Bookmaster. Photo: David Dalton

10 Showing Dachshunds

Pets on show
Betty Munt

There are many different kinds of shows; and most show Dachshunds, believe it or not, are pets. There are several different types of dog show, but here we will deal with the two main groups: open and championship shows.

Having purchased your puppy you will not be permitted to show it until it is six months old, so you have time to at least part train your dog. I hasten to add that few judges expect too much from a minor puppy, so try not to be too despondent if your pup does misbehave.

Betty Munt

Overall condition

Take care to observe the proper preliminaries concerning good care and management. Your dog must be in good health and trim condition, and fairly confident with other people and dogs. It must be neither too fat nor too lean, with good muscle, developed by proper walking and exercise. The pads on its feet must be hardened, the nails trimmed neatly, and the best nails are usually worn to the correct level by a mere tipping of the nail and allowing the pavement to do the rest. Soft grass and romping in the fields are not good enough; your dog must be road walked. So you see, achieving all this two days before a show is impossible.

Particular attention must be paid to your dog's diet and such treats as biscuits, cake, potato crisps and chocolate are forbidden, as are all snacks between meals. Treats may be offered as a form of reward and these might consist of a treated pig's ear, a skin bone, or chew.

'Stand!'

The 'musts' for a show dog are temperament and showmanship; without either your dog will get nowhere. Many champions in the ring have obvious faults and at best can only be considered mediocre. What they do possess is the ability to show their hearts out. The same might be said for handlers; a good dog can be ruined by bad handling and a mediocre dog enhanced beyond recognition by a talented handler.

Training your puppy to stand takes patience, from both dog and handler. From as early as a few weeks, this must be treated as a routine part of its normal care. With a very young puppy, five minutes twice a day should be enough to begin with. Stand your puppy on a non-slip surface and groom it gently with a soft brush. Use your voice to encourage, praise and reward your puppy when it gets it right. Your voice is your greatest asset. Never, repeat never, show impatience. Of course a young puppy will sit down; that's no big deal, all puppies do it. Let it sit a while and concentrate on its head and shoulders. Run your hands along its back, hold its head steady and then place two fingers below its tail and gently lift it onto its back legs. Place your pup in the show stance continuing to talk to it gently.

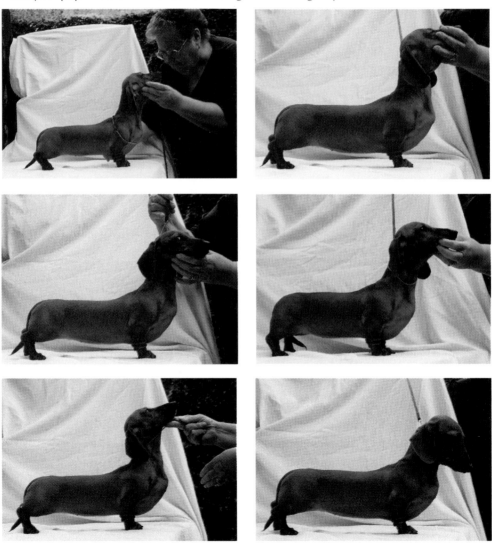

Betty Munt and soon-to-be-Ch Pipersvale Exclusive (see page 70)
demonstrate advanced ring training.
Ch Pipersvale Exclusive is a perfect Schneid red.

The word *Stand* is the key word here. This will not happen overnight, so when you feel yourself becoming frustrated and impatient – that's the time to stop.

When your puppy becomes more confident, you can be a little firmer, but always finish with a hug and an assurance that it's 'the cleverest dog that ever came out of a doggery'.

Ringcraft classes

When your puppy has had all its vaccinations, is used to its collar and lead, and can walk confidently by your side, you can take its training a step further. Ringcraft classes are good for all manner of things. They accustom your dog to the sight, sound and smell of other dogs: in effect, the atmosphere that is exclusive to the show ring. There are ringcraft classes in most towns and these are ideal, although they should not be confused with obedience training.

The whole ambience of a ringcraft class can be confusing and frightening to a new recruit, whatever its age. The purpose of such training is for dog and handler, so you too must be prepared to learn.

Do not expect too much too soon. Let it be enough for your dog (and you!) to sit and watch from the ringside for a couple of weeks. When you are both confident, by all means join in the fun.

Between ringcraft classes, encourage your friends and relations to examine your dog's bite. Few dogs enjoy having their top lip lifted to expose their teeth, so gently does it.

A word of caution is called for here. Avoid those class members who allow their dogs to be out of control on a long lead while they themselves are enjoying a chin-wag. The keyword here is concentration, and that applies equally when you are showing your dog in the proper ring.

Precautions

Certain things can be done between ring classes. For instance, do start taking your dog with you in the car, thus accustoming it to the motion – and to that strange animal that growls under the bonnet. Also, get your dog used to travelling in a cage. Never confine your dog in its travelling cage as a punishment. Try placing the cage in the living area and put your dog in it for its afternoon nap. If you leave the cage door open at other times you will soon find your dog retires to it of its own accord.

Some dog shows are *benched*. This simply

Good training: Ch Radclyffe Corvus standing on her own, without a lead.

means that benches are provided for your dogs and equipment. Each exhibit is allocated its own area. Some people place their dog, in its cage, on the bench. If the other dogs are particularly noisy, thus upsetting your dog, you can place a light blanket over his cage. This will afford your dog the privacy it needs.

At the show

At six months old your puppy is eligible for showing. It is not advisable to show a puppy if it is not ready. It is better by far to hold back for a few months than to have a frightened and overawed little dog. It should also be noted that dogs and puppies can, and often do, become tired. Some championship shows are held outdoors and, if you add up travelling time and a long day out, the handler as well as the dog will be exhausted by the end of the day.

All shows, whatever their class, are advertised, and the best places to find notification of these are the dog papers. As I have already said, the two main papers are *Dog World* and *Our Dogs*. These weekly publications can be ordered from any newsagent.

In general, shows do not accept entries on the day. Each show has a closing date and all entries should be posted before that date. It is a wise precaution to keep all cheque or postal order stubs, and all entrants should retain some kind of 'proof of posting'.

At some shows (not all) the exceptions to pre-paid entries are junior handling classes. These are judged between the official classes, usually according to the age of the entrant. The handlers rather than the dogs are judged.

After telephoning or sending by post for an entry form you will discover that there are various definitions for each class and the rules are clearly written. It is not wise to enter a puppy in a class too advanced for its age and experience. Better by far to progress through each class as your dog matures.

- *Minor Puppy* is reserved for dogs of six months and not exceeding nine calendar months of age on the first day of the show.
- *Puppy* is for dogs of six months and not exceeding twelve months of age on the first day of the show.

Whether they go by age or show wins, the subsequent classes should be entered as the dog becomes eligible for that class. There is little point in trying to show a raw puppy against champions and experienced show animals.

The place to start is the open show, and many experienced exhibitors use these shows as a kind of ringcraft class. They are fun shows where some very useful experience can be gained by both handler and dog.

Ring etiquette

Always arrive in good time. Find the exercise area and allow your dog to stretch its legs and relieve itself. Travelling with a few plastic bags is a good idea, as these will enable you to lift any toilet matter your dog may leave behind. I'm sure that you'll agree it's nice to be nice.

Find out what ring you are in and then settle your dog down comfortably. You can buy a programme and find your dog entered there with name of owner, breeder and date of birth.

Scottish Kennel Club Show 1980 – judge Joe McCauley with CC winners
Margaret Turner with Ch Maricture Black Modiste and Eileen Wood with Ch Woddric Idealist.

Beside your entry you will find a ring number, and this is the number under which you will show your dog. When the ring steward calls your class, you will tell him or her your number. You will then be given a card with the number printed on it. This must be attached to your arm or chest. You may use a safety pin, or most shows sell special little pins with a grip for the card board. Enquire at the secretary's table.

Next you line up with the other exhibitors and, if your dog is a Miniature, you will place it on the scales when asked to do so. Most shows have scales with an 5kg (11lb) weight, hence the term bumping the scales. The scales must not go down, which would indicate that your dog was over the limit. Some shows have scales which give a reading, but this is not strictly necessary. If you think your dog is bordering on the 5kg maximum it is permissible to remove its collar and lead. It is not always realised that a collar and lead can weigh up to 85g, which can make all the difference.

Watch, learn, and concentrate. Take note of the procedures. When the last dog has been weighed in and the line has re-established itself, stand your dog for the judge to look the class over. At this point some judges vary the procedure, and you must watch carefully for what is expected of you. Some may ask you to walk once or twice around the ring before asking the first in line to present their dog on the table to be examined (gone over). When asked to do so you will approach the table, standing to the back of the table or side-on to the judge. At no time must you put yourself between the dog and the judge, blocking the judge's view. You will then stand your dog to its best advantage.

The judge will take a long view of the dog for outline and a general impression before approaching the table. He or she will then run hands over the dog, checking, in the case of a male, that it has two testicles, examining the mouth for bite and the correct teeth and checking that they are clean and free from tartar. The judge will consider such things as leathers (ears), forefront and spring of rib, temperament, coat, eyes, and feet – in general, everything that makes a good animal sound. When the judge is satisfied he or she will ask you to move the dog.

The judge will tell you where to walk your dog. You may be asked to walk your dog in the shape of a triangle, then once, or even twice, straight up and down the central mat. When you have completed this course you will finish by standing your dog before the judge. Once satisfied, the judge will thank you and indicate that you should return to the back of the line up.

If you have entered for more than one class under the same judge, and the judge has already gone over your dog, he or she will not have to do so again. A dog that has already been seen will stand with all other 'seen' dogs on the opposite side of the ring. When the judge has seen all the newcomers the steward will indicate that 'seen' dogs should join the others in the class.

Before making the final choice the judge may ask you all to do yet another circle of the ring. He will then, by number, pick out those he has chosen for first, second, third, and sometimes fourth, which is usually the one chosen as Highly Commended. The rest of the class then leave the ring.

At this point the judge may well rearrange those chosen. Either way, first and second will remain in the ring while the judge writes up notes on the dogs.

Some *dos* and *don'ts*

Do give your fellow exhibitors plenty of elbow room. If you think your dog is being crowded, politely ask the other owner to move up or down a space.

Concentrate on your dog, one eye on the dog and the other on any directive the judge may give. If you have a waiting period when the judge is going over and walking the dogs ahead of you, let your own dog relax. If it is overawed or needs comfort you may pick it up and stroke it for a while.

After the weigh-in the judge might indicate that he or she wants you to walk around the ring in line with the other dogs. Keep a good pace, neither rushing whoever is ahead of you nor slacking off so that you are trailing. Your dog will be judged on its drive, its presence and its topline on the move in comparison with the other dogs.

A word of warning: all dogs have an extra sensory power. If you are nervous, anxious, unhappy or irritated, then be sure that these feelings will travel down the lead like electricity. Relax, and be happy. Encourage your dog, and let everything be fun. Try to keep everything in proportion. At the end of the day you will still be taking the best dog home, whatever decision the judge makes. A judge's opinion is only one person's opinion and, while these people are chosen for their knowledge of the breed, very often the decision comes down to 'type'. Different judges may like different types of Dachshund, and we don't necessarily have to agree.

Later on, when you come to know and recognise your fellow exhibitors, you will discover that even those who appear to be unbeatable have their bad days. Try to give credit where it's due. Some exhibitors have been showing for a good many years. They are experienced and many of the dogs they are currently exhibiting are fashionable. These people are well known to those in the ring, and also to the judge. It will be known that they are consistent winners, that dogs shown under their affix will be quality stock, and you will have a long, hard pull to match them. Be gracious in defeat. Congratulate the winner – and mean it. Be equally gracious when you win. Bad manners in the ring are not tolerated and will be remembered.

Don't chat to whoever is standing beside you in the ring. Be pleasant without breaking the other's concentration. Never talk to the judge unless you are spoken to. Answer all questions without additional information. If you have any questions for the judge, or thanks for your win, these must be saved until after the judge has finished judging. Never question a judge's decision; it will do you no good. The judge's decision is final.

If your dog disgraces itself, ask the steward for the mop and pail, or sawdust and shovel. Clean up your own dog's mess.

If you are not sure how to proceed when you have won, do seek advice from the secretary or steward. You won't be the first exhibitor to go home happy with a first only to discover you were eligible for Best in Show. If in doubt, ask, always remembering that the time for socialising is after the class has been judged.

Your dog will have been prepared well in advance of the show. As already indicated, it will have been groomed and bathed, its nails well trimmed and ears cleaned. If you attend to all these things several days before the show, the dog will have plenty of time to calm down and relax.

For the actual show a tackle box is very useful and should contain the following items for your dog:

- brushes and combs
- scissors
- nailclippers
- cotton wool balls and nappy wipes
- spare lead
- pre-packed dog treats
- bottle of water
- dish
- large towel for your dog to stand on for his last minute grooming
- pump spray with water should you need to dampen its coat. (No other additives should be used. All cosmetic aids which might change or alter the structure or colour of the dog's coat are punishable offences.)
- poop-scoops and plastic bags

For your own comfort you should consider:

- a folding chair
- sandwiches or pre-packed salads in plastic containers
- large thermos flasks for soup, coffee or tea
- a stout pair of wellington boots
- waterproofed coat and hat or scarf
- a heavy-knit cardigan, jumper or overcoat
- a waterproofed hat or scarf

(The heavier items can be left in the car if not needed)

What to wear

Last but not least, do resist all urges to join the 'Scruff Brigade'. These people can be seen at all shows. They think it is fashionable or makes some kind of statement. 'I'm totally absorbed in my dogs so I can't be bothered (simply don't have the time or interest) to smarten myself up.'

If there is any question about what to wear, keep it simple. Well pressed trousers or a skirt are ideal. Frills and flounces do not go down well, but good, plain, sporting-type clothes are never out of place. Consider the colour of your dog; a dark dog will not stand out against a

After a hard day's showing…

black background. Shoes are important. Stiletto heels might look good but they are out of place in the ring. Leather soles on slippery indoor venues are a hazard; rubber or crêpe soled shoes are comfortable and less risky. Whatever you can afford, clean, well-pressed and simple should be the rule.

Showing Standard Smooths
Margaret Turner (Marictur)

How easy it is to forget how daunting our first show can be and the awful mistakes we've all made at one time or another. When pausing to consider how I could write something to encourage newcomers to the breed, I had time to remember our beginnings – the genesis of the Marictur Dachshunds.

In the beginning, in fact throughout the whole of my childhood, several mongrel dogs graced our home but, by the time I became a teenager, I knew that one day I would own a Dachshund. This half-conscious train of thought, I think in hindsight, was influenced by my father who, as a sailor, made regular visits to Germany. His stories about Germany and his admiration of the Smooth-haired Dachshunds he saw there coloured my imagination and ambition. In 1970, when our old and much-loved terrier died, I decided to have no more dogs. This resolve lasted all of four months. I heard about a litter of Standard Smooth-haired Dachshunds bred by Rosemary Miller and went along to see them. I bought Keidon Kassandra (Tanya) as a pet and brought the tiny six-week-old puppy home with me. She was gorgeous.

A few months later I saw a notice advertising a local dog show and, as I now had a real pedigree dog, I decided to go along. I was thrilled when, in spite of my ineptitude as a handler, I was handed a fourth prize. More to the point, several people commented favourably about Tanya. I really enjoyed myself, and I was hooked!

Despite my heavy work commitments I began to attend an ever-wider radius of shows most weekends and found a wealth of help. Tanya's breeder and many other exhibitors were most helpful and it opened up a new world I had hitherto not known existed. I watched, listened and learned how to train Tanya properly. Because she loved food, she was relatively easy to train. Came the day when, at the East Yorkshire Dachshund Club Show, we won two first prizes. What a fantastic weekend that was. Later we managed to qualify for Crufts.

We went to the canine show of all canine shows with Tanya's breeder, Rosemary Miller, and stayed overnight, making a weekend of it. Tanya was entered in Postgraduate in which there were 13 other exhibits. Then, after a heart-stopping finish, she was placed first. I felt that the world could hold no more. We also got £4 in prize money.

After that Tanya was a very consistent open show winner and gave me endless pleasure for many years. My only sorrow was that we never got a puppy from her.

In 1972 I had bought another Standard Smooth-haired Dachshund for showing. Ch Murantia Janine Marictur (Gypsy) was a very different type from Tanya. At eight months old she was small and so slow to mature that a judge once asked me if she really was a Standard. She was also much harder to train and manage than Tanya. In fact, it took more than two years before I felt I was really getting somewhere with her.

Ch Murantia Janine Marictur, 1974.

Margaret Turner with Ch Murantia Janine Marictur, Bitch
CC winner, Crufts 1976.

By this time I was well into championship shows. At the Scottish Kennel Club, Kelvin Hall, Glasgow in 1974 we won the postgraduate and limit classes and, as I was crouching over my dog in the final line-up, I was handed the CC. Friends around the ring said my face was a picture; I lost my balance and almost fell over. That was my first CC, an occasion I shall never forget.

Gypsy became a champion, winning her fourth CC at Crufts in 1976. There was a down side: a few people who felt that I had done too much too soon, that inevitable minority that is part and parcel of any competitive sport. It is a side we must all recognise but not emulate. Such attitudes are bad sportsmanship and do not reflect well on the breed - any breed, come to that. Becoming a part of the dog-scene proper I have learned to cope with it. After all, criticism is often the accolade of success.

The next 'first' for me was breeding my first litter. Delivered by caesarean section – three puppies – mother patently disinterested – owner afraid she might kill them – owner running around like a headless chicken – I was terrified! However, a succession of good friends breached the gap, giving me advice, showing me how to latch a whelp onto a teat, holding mum's head well out of the way. They demonstrated how to bottle feed, use a heat lamp, and all else that was necessary. What a stressful time that was. After two days and nights my husband and I were dazed from lack of sleep. But Gypsy gradually became aware that she was a mother. We gently introduced her to her puppies and all settled down normally

Many years and much water has gone under the bridge since then. I have learned a lot about people, myself and managing my dogs. Such things as improving my stock, most of all about not keeping more dogs than I can give attention to.

Over the years I have been proud to learn that my Dachshunds have become well-known for their excellent coat condition. I have been asked many time what I gave them. The well-known Judge Bobby James once ruffled the back of one of my bitches' coats in a championship stakes class and even bent down to sniff at it. I told him that finish came from within, and he just nodded and smiled.

Skin condition I have found is mostly inherited, but can be greatly enhanced by proper feeding. I do not use a lot of supplements, just an occasional course of halibut oil capsules and brewers yeast tablets in the first year and sometimes in the winter months after that. Any odd little coat problems are almost always put right by good old Bob Grass' skin care ointment, a very old-fashioned remedy which, in my opinion, has never been bettered.

Margaret Turner with Ch Marictur Easter Music, 1982. Photo: David Freeman

I rarely bath my dogs. Instead I brush them and rub them over with a dampened cloth. Neither do I believe in high-protein foods; I give them meat and biscuit, with a little 'complete' to top up if necessary.

I have never had outdoor kennels and believe that all smooth-coated Dachshunds benefit from being house-bred and reared in warmer conditions.

Of all my champions the one I rate highest is Ch Marictur Easter Music (Bebe),

Ch Marictur Easter Music.

for type, size, bone, ribbing and elegance. She had very little tan markings and I must admit to admiring 'sooty' looking Dachshunds. In my opinion they look more elegant than the more clearly defined black-and-tans. Bebe won most consistently for me, including a CC at Crufts in 1985. She was a wonderful mother and was dam to three champions, continuing to win well into Veteran. At the age of 9 she won Reserve Best in Show at a very large Open Show, Reserve Best in Show at The Scottish Dachshund Club at 10, and won her last Veteran Class at The West Riding Dachshund Club show at 12, before retiring. At the time of writing this she is still alive at 15, and queen of our house.

Because of work commitments I have not bred many litters, preferring to show one dog for several years. Also, I have never owned any colour other than black-and-tan, but this is not because I am biased against other colours; in fact, I greatly admire both red and chocolate.

Over the years, like many Standard Dachshund owners, we have had to face the problems of stock becoming too big. With size in mind we have deliberately chosen dogs with a view to achieving correct size, substance and elegance.

Ch Sontag Super Sleuth and Ch Easter Music produced Ch Marictur Mr Moto at 11.8kg (26lb) and Ch Marictur Modesty Blaise was 10kg (22lb). My present dog, Ch Martictur Marriot, weighs 11.8kg. I have to say that a little over size does not necessarily prevent me from giving high awards when judging, as long as size is in proportion to bone, hard condition, type and elegance. Having said that, we must not encourage overweight dogs of 13.6kg (30lb) or more in our Smooths and, above all, our dogs must retain their elegance.

Temperament is another problem in Standard Smooths and is very much a hit and miss predicament, something very hard to breed for. One simply cannot guarantee good temperament in puppies, even when breeding from a dam and sire who are not nervous. Most people are conscious of these problems and have to consider temperament when breeding for type and quality.

Now that I have retired my aim for the future is to ontinue more or less as I am. I like my dogs around the house, where they are free to sit anywhere they wish (unless one of our ladies is in season), and I must say that the only time I yearn for an outside kennel is when my puppies are about six weeks old. I would love to breed a nice red, or a chocolate, and I may try, using an outcross, although line breeding, especially half brother and sister, has always worked well for me in the past.

Unfortunately, a considerable problem in Standard Smooths at this time is the dearth of young stock in the show ring, especially in the dog classes, where entries have dropped to one, two, or none. Consequentially, there are few up-and-coming stud dogs to choose from. Registration with The Kennel Club was as low as 212 in 1995, which practically makes us a rare breed. We have had more than our share of multiple CC winners over the years, but I do not feel they are entirely to blame for the apparent lack of interest in the show ring.

We end on an optimistic note, however. There is a growing body of opinion among exhibitors that the development and formation of a club for Standard and Miniature Smooths would bring us into line with the other coated varieties, who all have their own clubs. This may provide a point of stimulus and regenerate interest in our variety, a variety which has often been refered to as the blueprint of the breed.

Showing Miniature Longs
Betty Cole-Hamilton (Beltrim)

If anyone had asked me in my younger days what breed of dog I would least like to own, the answer might well have been, 'A Dachshund!'

I remember well my very first dog, a charming and much-loved black Cocker called Jane. Also, during the Second World War, I was lucky enough to 'inherit' the Company dog of the staff-car drivers in Chester. That was Penny, a truly wonderful broken-coated old-fashioned terrier, the most intelligent and devoted animal imaginable and a joyous companion in those war-weary days. Yes, those were the sort of dogs for me – not a Dachshund!

But these little hounds have a way of proving us wrong! Occasionally my army duties would enable me to stay with my Hanbury-Sparrow relatives in Church Stretton, where my cousin Brian lived with his pack of 20+ Miniature Longs (of the Yeld affix). In my mind's eye I can still picture the sea of waving tails around him, but at that stage they meant nothing to me, or I to them.

However, I had reckoned without Jenny, a delightful aptly-named little chocolate-and-tan, Robsvarl Jenny Wren. In the inimitable way that Dachshunds set out to captivate those resistant to their charms, so it was that Jenny made me her target. She adopted me at first sight as her property and never left me during my stay, sitting on my knee, sleeping on my bed at night, to the complete exclusion of her 'own' people. The same happened throughout my subsequent and infrequent visits. I still cannot explain this after all these years in the breed, but that is what happened, and of course I was suitably flattered and began to think vaguely that perhaps there was something to be said for these funny little dogs.

Even so, some years later and married with a young family, it was only after a disastrous experience with a Cocker puppy that I wrote to Brian to ask whether he had an older youngster available with the temperament we wanted. In due course I collected Susie (Springmount Japonica, a daughter of Ch Marcus of Mornyvarna ex Ch Primrosepatch Juliette) off the night train at Waverley Station and, although Brian had warned me that, being

Ch Don Basilio of Mallards (Leo).

10 months old, she might take a day or two to settle down, within minutes of her arrival she was queening it with the whole family in our double bed! She was the best £10's worth of my life and the start of a love-affair which has lasted for 45 years, so far.

Susie was later mated to Brian's dog Peregrine of the Yeld, and through their progeny I have been left a lasting legacy by his grandmother, the little charmer that started it all, Robsvarl Jenny Wren.

From the above mating there was one particularly nice bitch puppy whom I called Caroline of Beltrim, the first to carry my affix. Considering my very unprofessional efforts at handling, she did well in the ring and as a brood bitch, and gradually our little 'kennel of house pets' increased in number.

It soon became clear that, as the only Miniature Long-hair breeder in Scotland at that time, unless I wished to continue sending bitches South every time they were to be mated I would have to start looking around for a suitable stud dog of my own – which brings us to the story of Don Basilio of Mallards, illustrating only too well the pitfalls that can befall the novice owner and how a good dog can rise above them regardless!

From the start I particularly wanted my stud dog to have a bold temperament, as well as good looks. By following show reports in the dog press I noticed that Mrs Sybil Gale (later Rybarczyk) had dogs which particularly seemed to excel in these attributes. Her current show dog was sired by Ch Springmount Madrigal, a beautiful dog I had already used successfully on my stock, the dam being Sybil's own Ch Fricassee of Mallards.

When a repeat litter of this mating was advertised in 1958, consisting of three red dogs, one black-and-tan, and a red bitch, I wrote off post-haste hoping for one of the red dogs, my stock at that time being mainly black-and-tan. Alas, I was too late: all three reds were bespoken, leaving the red bitch and the black-and-tan dog. 'But,' said Sybil, 'I think the black-and-tan is the pick of the litter.' How right she proved to be! Although the little red bitch did do some winning, I never heard any more of the red dogs. The gods were definitely smiling on me when I decided to have Don Basilio of Mallards (Leo to his friends), colour notwithstanding. Sybil wrote of him, 'The dog is very lovely, with a magnificent head, dark almond eyes and wonderful feet,' also saying that she would gladly keep him for me to collect on a forthcoming trip to London.

I don't know how Sybil managed to contrive it but, when husband Dick and I eventually arrived at her house in Kenton and rang the bell, the door seemed to open of its own accord and we were greeted by an enchanting waggy little black person who welcomed us into the house. We were thrilled by Leo's personality and appearance, and bore him off triumphantly. We had to attend a luncheon gathering at the Paddington Hotel before travelling North, and even the head waiter succumbed to his charms and let us smuggle him into the dining-room with us (strictly against the rules even in those days). We had no box or crate with us, but he gave no trouble at all, either at lunch or on the journey home.

Our 'girls' were delighted with him, and he was quickly accepted into the canine family. He was very self-possessed and confident from the start. Even at that early stage he possessed a debonair panache that lasted throughout his life.

Leo grew in fits and starts. At one time his wonderful masculine head seemed much too big for his body (reminding me of a handsome tadpole), but eventually things began to come together and I entered him for the autumn Scottish Kennel Club's Championship Show (no CCs then for Miniature Longs) under Dr Stephen Young. He immediately spotted Leo's potential and gave him his class and Best of Breed. A month later under Mrs Littmoden at Birmingham National he won his three classes and the Reserve CC. I took him to Crufts in February 1959 under Mrs H M Roberts, and as I boarded the night train I knew I was hatching flu. I lived for 36 hours on whisky and aspirin, but we came home with firsts in both his classes, Puppy and Junior.

Leo was a joy to handle, being an exceptionally confident showman and mover. With his outstanding head and front, good length, bone and feet, lovely straight coat and air of quality and style, he was hard to overlook at a time when Miniature Long-hairs as a breed were still very mixed in type. He gained his Junior Warrant, and then came our trip to Blackpool with Miss Cook.

Miss Cook was then very much a grande dame in the world of Dachshunds, whereas I was very small fry indeed, and I felt extremely honoured to be travelling with her. In those days the Blackpool Society ran a little shuttle for exhibitors between the station and Stanley Park, and I arranged with Miss Cook to meet her at the station for our return train at 4.00 pm. This I did, unfortunately overlooking the fact that in the meantime Mr Buck had awarded Leo the dog CC – and Best of Breed had not yet been judged! I was deeply mortified when I realised my terrible gaffe, entirely due to my ignorance of the big-time routine, and I am ashamed to this day to have to relate that Don Basilio was awarded Best of Breed in his absence. Things were more relaxed in those days. All the same, nothing could spoil the thrill of winning my first CC.

Leo mated his first bitch at seven months (while nobody was looking), but predictably there were no puppies. At the start of his serious stud career he was far too enthusiastic and flamboyant, and it was very much a hit and miss affair. A friend brought a bitch to him three mornings running, and the best we could achieve was a mating lasting about one second on the third day – resulting in eight puppies! However, his technique did improve, and in June 1960 he went back to stay with Sybil and be mated to her Ch Bijou of Mallards, and also for Sybil to handle him at Windsor Championship Show, where Mrs Gatheral was the judge. Sybil subsequently wrote *It is a joy to have Leo. He is the sweetest dog I know. He and Bijou met for a brief moment in the ring yesterday when they were challenging each other for Best of Breed. Paul had my instructions to keep at least five yards away from Bijou. Mrs Gatheral wanted to see them both together, so I said that she had better not, or she might see more than she bargained for!* Bijou went Best of Breed and Leo returned with his second CC.

I had been planning to take him to the City of Birmingham Show that summer under Mrs Buck, who had liked him so much as a youngster, but about two months before the show we had a major crisis. Leo was operated on for a (mercifully) benign tumour of the bowel. He returned from the vet with his side shaved, a large stitched wound and as thin as a rake. This did not prevent him from ripping out his stitches at the earliest opportunity, leaving a gaping wound with edges too jagged to be re-stitched. For about three weeks it did not seem to heal at all. Then at the last it did begin to mend, but it was touch-and-go whether he would be ready for Birmingham.

By the day of the show the wound had healed completely and the hair had grown in, looking black but not its full length, so we decided to risk it. In the event we were incredibly lucky. Rain caused the Miniature Longs to be judged in a wet-weather tent where there was less light, and the 'patch' was on the side away from the judge as I tabled him. He was pulled out second for a final turn around the ring and then signalled to go first. My husband said he had never seen me run so fast, and I believe him! Leo won his qualifying CC and Best of Breed, our first champion - beyond my wildest dreams.

Leo subsequently won two more CCs with Best of Breed and numerous other awards, including Best in Show at the Scottish Dachshund Club's Open Show. He was also joint top-winning Miniature Long-haired dog for 1960. He had many glowing critiques, but I particularly treasure a short one from Miss Tilney, who wrote: *Substance, symmetry and soundness, I consider this dog quite outstanding*, which says it all. The credit goes to his breeder, Sybil, who did so much to help me throughout his career.

Leo became a great stud force, producing champion, CC and Res CC winning offspring. All of my Beltrims descend from him and hopefully inherit some of his quality and soundness. Most of all it was his big-dog personality and lively, affectionate nature which made this beautiful champion such a pleasure and an honour to own. His rôle as companion and friend fully equalled his success in the show ring and combined to make him a dog I shall never forget or cease to be grateful for.

As advice has already been given elsewhere regarding teeth, feet and general care, I propose to confine myself to a few generalities which may be of help to the novice exhibitor.

Although a healthy, well-fed and regularly exercised Miniature Long should should carry a good 'bloom' on its coat, a bath before a show will almost certainly add that extra touch of glamour that we hope will catch the judge's eye. It will also provide an opportunity to put the finishing touch to the nails, much easier to trim after soaking! A bath is doubly to be recommended if your dog is not in full coat: it will provide a little extra bulk to the remaining coat and will at least make it look clean and glossy.

It makes sense to give experimental baths well before the pup's debut in the show ring to determine which shampoo best suits him and how many days to allow for the coat to settle; it is surprising how the results differ. I have often used human shampoos to good effect.

Very occasionally, a dog may look better without a bath, usually when the coat has a tendency to wave. It is very much a question of trial and error, but well worth the effort to achieve an exhibit in sparkling condition on the day.

Apart from the feet, I did not 'tailor' my dogs as a general rule; since they were hounds I preferred them to look as natural as possible, once I had got them looking their best as described above. However, sometimes a judicious thinning (finger and thumb) of excess hair under the neck can improve the outline, particularly where there is a suspicion of 'stuffiness'. After a bath the ear-fringes and feathering will have a good straight appearance, and a quick comb here and there will be all that is necessary before entering the ring.

For most of my Miniatures I used a narrow ribbon lead which I could slacken over the shoulder when tabling or in the line-up; this helps to set off the neck and shoulder placement. The type of lead is a matter of personal preference and many prefer a fine choke chain; at all events, avoid a thick collar and lead, as these do not look right on a Miniature Long.

Ch Minutist Casino, bred by Mrs N Parsons and owned by Betty Cole-Hamilton. Photo: C M Cooke

Unfortunately, even the most careful preparation cannot always win prizes, but at least you go home knowing you have done your best for your dog and learnt a little from experts, and there is always another day – and a chance of that coveted big green card.

Showing Standard Wires
Valerie Skinner (Ritterburg)

As well as working with Dachshund Rescue, I am the owner, breeder and exhibitor of Standard Wire-haired Dachshunds, and my affix is Ritterburg.

My story began in 1959, with a Standard Smooth-haired Dachshund given to me by my husband soon after we were married. Of course, I was an absolute 'novice': in fact, I had never owned a dog before. However, the breeder assured me that he was good enough to show and, after winning at sanction, limit and small open shows, I was truly bitten by the 'show bug'.

In 1960 I acquired a smooth-haired bitch, along with my affix Ritterburg. After that I exhibited Smooths at Open level for about seven years. Looking back, we didn't go to championship shows until we had served what might be termed as a sort of apprenticeship; we worked our way up the ladder.

In 1963 we bought a Long-haired bitch and bred our first Long-haired champion who, in 1973, became Ch Ritterburg Rhine Romanesque, and went on to gain six CCs and two Reserve CCs.

Although I enjoyed my time with Smooths and Longs (and by this time we even had two Miniature Long-hairs) our greatest love has to be our Standard Wire-haired Dachshunds, who came into our lives in the shape of a little red bitch, Red Rosette of Ritterburg, in 1976. She was a real charmer, so full of love, fun and character and so eager to please. That's when we decided that this was the variety for us.

Innishmaan Ebony Eyes of Ritterburg was born in 1978 and, while she was never a CC winner herself, she produced three champions. In her first litter, when taken to Ch Fraserwood Neon Star, she produced our lovely Ch Ritterburg Briar (Top bitch for 1982 and the winner of

12 CCs). Out of her second litter, sired by William of Ellesmere, came Ch Ritterburg Dark Destiny (Top Wire-haired in 1984 and 1985, with 17 CCs). Then in her third litter she produced Ch Ritterburg Dark Dolly.

Ch Dark Destiny was then mated to Ch Verwill Oakmaster, producing Ch Dark Dynasty (Top Wire-hair in1988 with 12 CCs). Sadly, this bitch proved to be sterile, so we bought in Flaming Katy (Daxene Kinsman ex Ritterburg Red Briar). She soon became a champion, winning 14 CCs and BOB at Crufts in 1990, being in the last eight for the group. Sadly, she was difficult to breed from. So, buying Ritterburg Red Briar back, we mated her to Ch Andlouis Black Knight, who had 52 CCs. His grandsire and granddam were Ritterburgs, so the line was preserved. This mating produced our first ever dog champion, Ch Ritterburg Dark Duellist. He was top puppy in 1990, top sire in 1994, and top stud in 1995. After this he was mated to a daughter of Red Briar, giving us Ch Arminen Estella at Ritterburg (5 CCs). We have to say that Estella is a particular favourite of ours and has become very much a part of our family. She has such a delightful temperament, with so much love to give – and she actually sleeps on our bed (bless her little heart).

Our lovely Ch Andlouis Sorceress at Ritterburg, with 11 CCs and Top Wire-hair 1995, came from a litter sired by Ch Ritterburg Dark Duellist ex Andlouis Lady in Red (a full sister to Ch Andlouis Black Knight).

When planning a mating I like the pedigree lines to tie up. I look for a sire who will complement my bitch and improve or eradicate some fault – temperament must play a large part. I find half-sister to half-brother and granddaughter to grandsire particularly good matings. A good example of such line-breeding, tying up all my old lines, is Ch Arminen Estella at Ritterburg.

Valerie Skinner with Ch Arminen Estella at Ritterburg.
Photo: Shaun Flannery

Showing Miniature Wires
Jeff Horswell

The Miniature Wire was the last variety to arrive on these shores, making an impact shortly after the Second World War and gaining CC status in the late 1950s, so in many ways it is quite a new breed.

It was most fortunate that several of the early enthusiasts for this variety had already been successful in other Dachshund varieties. Perhaps this accounts for the fairly steady progress.

At first the dogs had a weight limit of 5.4kg (12lb), but with CC status this went down to 5kg (11lb) - a big, sudden drop from which the males took quite some time to recover. Indeed, the number of animals that grow on still causes problems. These animals can be very useful in a breeding programme, provided they are used

Ch Drakesleat Toot Sweet won the 1997 Hound Show Champion Bitch Stakes under Valerie Foss, handled by Jeff Horswell. Also Top Min Wire 1996, 97, BOB Crufts '96 and winner of three Hound groups at Championship shows.

sensibly. Close breeding seems to reduce size, but the breeder must be selective and know what he or she is doing when adopting this measure.

There were some good early imports. In those days inter-breeding was allowed, so other varieties could be used to improve the stock and widen the gene pool. Several lightweight Standard Wires were used, which back then meant about 6.3kg (14lb), as well as some top winning Miniature Smooths. Add the use of other varieties and the number of already successful Dachshund breeders taking the Miniature Wire on, and you will see why the breed did not take long for the best to be able to compete against their more established relations.

The Miniature Wire is a valuable part of the Dachshund family. It should look just like the very best Standard Smooth, but have a wire jacket and be under 5kg (11lb). It is not a separate breed and we should never use phrases like 'good front for a Miniature Wire' or accept anything less than we would in any of the other varieties. As with most small versions, there can always be a tendency to 'toyness'. Because of the cuteness of the Miniature Wire there is an inclination to breed something 'toy-like'. This practice should not be encouraged. Indeed, earlier Breed Standards expressly warned against this danger. The Dachshund is a hound, and the Miniature Wire should look as if it could go out and do a day's work.

Nature is always ready to play tricks on breeders of livestock. When you are breeding

145

smaller animals not all parts of the body necessarily reduce in size at the same rate. For example, upper arms tend to reduce in size quicker than shoulder blades. Eyes tend to go rounder rather than maintaining a desirable almond shape. All Miniatures tend to have rounder eyes than their Standard cousins, and shorter upper arms is more of a problem in the Miniature, although it is far from uncommon in other breeds.

Breeders need to be aware of these facts, but must never accept that, just because it happens, they should accept round eyes and short upper arms. Both these faults must be bred out and perfection should always be the goal: anything less must be improved on.

The Dachshund is a breed that can easily lend itself to exaggeration. We want a long, low hound. In an effort to win shows there can be a temptation to breed as low as possible and as long as possible. Neither is correct. We still see far too many Miniature Wires with chests too low and over-long backs. Exhibitors can be heard complaining at outdoor shows that the grass is too long for their dogs to show off their movement. It may be the dog that is wrong, not the grass.

To breed, or even to judge a breed to the highest standard, you must understand the job of work for which the Dachshund was originally created. Keep that at the front of your mind and always ask, 'Could it do a day's work? Lowness to ground means not too tall. It does not mean an exaggerated chest nearly touching the ground. Such a dog would not last in the field. A Dachshund must have legs. If the keel comes below the wrist it is a serious fault, not a virtue.

The length of the Dachshund is in the body, not the back. The length from sternum to rump should be twice the height at the withers for perfect balance. If the dog is made correctly in front with long shoulders and upper arm at a 90°angle, up to one third of its length should be in front of the forelegs. Correct angulation will give the body length required. A short loin is essential for strength.

Ideally the topline on the Dachshund should not be flat, and the neck should not be set at a 90° angle to the topline. The neck should have a good arch to it and flow into rather high withers. The lumber region is then straight, with the loins slightly arched for strength.

Movement is an indication of correct construction. Ours should be a free-moving breed with a long stride. The Miniature Wire should move with purpose across the ring, not breaking stride at every clump of grass. The Miniature is not like a wound-up toy mouse and the handler should have to pace out to keep up with the dog, not the other way round.

Legs should move forward in a straight line and should not cross from front to rear. If they do then there is a real problem. The correct construction, which includes correct muscle as well as the length and placement of bone, could not possibly cross.

Fortunately, Dachshund breeders have always been interested in construction above all else, never the head or colour of the breed. Having said that, a good head is essential to a working hound and helps stamp the correct hound type.

There is a wide range of colours in the Miniature Wire. In the 1970s the vast majority were red. Now the brindle seems to be dominant. Black-and-tan and chocolate are often seen, as are dapples. A great many of the earlier Dachshunds were dapples, so perhaps it is surprising that there are not more of them. On the whole, breeders tend not to have any colour prejudices. Nor do they devote much of their time to breeding for certain colours – rightly so in my opinion.

Eyes and ears are two of the most vulnerable areas of attack from the badger. To protect them the two essentials are 'terrier type' teeth and a length of muzzle to create distance between quarry and danger. It also helps to have the correct length of ear, which should not come past the nose, and eyes that do not bulge.

In the early days when we were trying to get the right construction, coats were of secondary concern. That is not to say that all the earlier dogs had bad coats – far from it. But in those early days, the late 1970s, soft and fluffy coats were quite often seen. These have improved greatly, and rarely do we see a really bad coat. Having said that, coats do vary.

Presentation has improved over the years, partly because we now understand more about preparing the coat for show. This is partly because the modern show scene is more competitive. The stripping and trimming of the coat has been dealt with by Elizabeth Fulton of the 'Bothlyn' affix in Chapter 9, and I cannot in all honesty improve on this. However, I will add a few words of caution for future judging. The Wire-haired coat can be sculpted to improve the shape of the dog and we should not be fooled by this practice. The dog should look smart, and from a distance must look like a Smooth. The best trimmers may leave you thinking that you like the effect, but from a distance it's almost impossible to see scissor marks.

So, how do we compare with our other Dachshund relatives – and indeed, can we compete with other hounds? The Miniature Wire is always a 'crowd-pleaser': the cute little face, wagging tail, bold head and defiant carriage, and free and flowing movement make it a winner with judges. This extrovert temperament is something we should breed for, as well as developing and encouraging it in our puppies. I think it is fair to say that the best in our breed do compete well against the best of any breed.

I have placed great emphasis on the fact that the Miniature Wire-haired Dachshund is first and foremost a hunting dog, not a lap-dog, although it will quite happily fill this role given the opportunity. It is a dog of German origin and the breed, especially the Wire, is still very popular in its native homeland. However, although we all started with the same basic stock, in the English-speaking world we have developed in a different direction from the rest of Europe. It is my hope that we keep an open mind and eventually produce an 'International' Dachshund.

In many ways the Miniature Wire is one of the best placed varieties to bridge this difference between standards, a gap that is not really so very great. The best in the United Kingdom could win high awards on the Continent – not my words, but those of one of Germany's top Dachshund authorities after a visit to Crufts.

A few years ago I attended an International Show in Scandinavia and I was glued to the Dachshund ring. The Best of Breed Miniature Wire (who won the Teckel Group that day) was a dream of a bitch. In my opinion, had I been able to bring her home, she would have been a very big winner in Great Britain. Yes, there are dogs over there that I was not keen on, as there are plenty here that do not please my eye; but the Breed Standards are very similar, so I wonder why the dogs are not? Who knows, if the quarantine laws are relaxed sometime in the future, we may be able to compete against each other. Think of the thrill of making a British dog into a German Champion. That would really be the icing on the cake.

The future of the breed is in the hands of the current generation of breeders. This is a breed that does breed 'true'. By using a dog that complements the bitch, progress can be made. I endorse the advice offered in the chapters on breeding in this book, and agree that it is not advisable to take a bitch to the nearest dog simply because he is handy. That is surely a move backwards in the Wire's evolution.

Breeders should always be critical of their own stock, thinking a generation or two ahead. Ask for advice, study pedigrees and consider the compatibility of both dog and bitch. Ask those experienced in the breed; by and large they are a helpful lot who will gladly pass on their expertise. Do listen and learn.

The Wire-Haired Dachshund is a wonderful variety, a functional hound and companion, and a loyal friend.

Tales of three winners

A day to remember

Dictated by Ch Aboutturn of Amberleigh (Tom to my friends) to Pam Evans (Amberleigh)
When Mum and I went to Crufts, we had an exciting time and the journey was spiced with adventure. Believe it or not (strictly against the rules) Mum smuggled me into the sleeper in a cardboard box marked: *FRAGILE. EGGS. WITH CARE.*

All went well until someone knocked at the door and asked to see Mum's ticket. While she was delving into her capacious handbag (more like a Santa Claus sack), I poked my head through the lid to check what was happening. Mum shoved me back inside and faked a coughing fit, whirling her arms around like a windmill. The ticket collector fled – probably afraid she was going bananas. Only then was I allowed out for an excellent roll on the hard, British Rail carpet. Mum laughed, saying that I looked like a Phoenix rising from the ashes, and that it had been a narrow squeak. I agreed, not wanting to show my ignorance.

After a good and undisturbed sleep we were on our way to my never-to-be-forgotten day of triumph. I can still hear the tremendous clapping for my lap of honour when I won first prize – it was absolutely deafening. Truly, a day to remember!

If at first..

Jim and Jean Sinclair (Cairnsilk)
... you don't succeed, try, try, and try again! The road to the top is paved with mischance and misadventure, and only those enthusiasts who have the stamina – stubbornness, for want of a better description – will make it to the top. This is why we have decided to tell you about 'Lisa' (Cairnsilk Black Diamond), our Miniature Long-haired.

Lisa was born in a litter of four in 1991. She was sired by Ch Helenium Lord of the Isles, winner of 12 CCs, who was in his turn sired by Crestwar Firecracker of Ringlingisle, owned by the late and much-revered Bob Gow. Lisa was out of our own Ringlingisle Midnight of Cairnsilk, who qualified for Crufts every year until we retired her; she too was bred by Bob Gow.

Jim and Jean Sinclair with Tobi (black-and-tan), Hans (Schneid red) and Lisa (black-and-tan).

From as early as four months old, Lisa showed promise, appearing more mature and bolder than her litter brothers and sister. She stood well on the table and showed every sign of wanting to show, a great asset in any dog intended for the ring. She also mixed well, showing quite happily for several friends who handled her.

Our excitement knew no bounds when we entered her in her first championship show at Blackpool and she was given a first in the puppy class by Mrs Betty Munt. Her critique was glowing and we basked in the reflected glory. Mrs Munt said of her: Super head, well placed shoulders, should have a good future! And, of course, this win also qualified her for Crufts.

The actual start of her 'off-the-table' syndrome came at a handling class. We were approached by a friend who asked if we would allow her little girl to handle Lisa in a junior handling competition. Of course, we were flattered and agreed, always anxious to encourage young hopefuls.

The day for the competition arrived, and we duly presented the child with Lisa, freshly groomed and looking her best. We took our seats at the ringside and prepared to enjoy the afternoon. Lisa walked and behaved impeccably and we were justifiably proud of her. When the time came, the little girl lifted Lisa up onto the table to be gone over by the judge.

It was then that disaster struck. Lisa caught sight of Jean at the ringside and joyfully made to bound off the table. Horrified, the child made a grab for Lisa, catching her by her rear legs. Lisa swung awkwardly, giving a heart-rending squeal of pain. The little girl was very near to tears as she watched Lisa limp over to where Jean and I were sitting. We comforted both dog and child, and honestly believed that no lasting damage had been done.

Physically, Lisa appeared fine. However, Dachshunds are intelligent animals and their memories are long. From then on she equated the judging table with pain and cowered away from any judge who came near her. It took us over a year to woo her confidence and assure her that the table was not a harmful place. There were times when we almost gave up hope that she would ever regain her assurance, but we persevered. At last we decided that it was now or never, and entered her for Bath Championship Show.

In hindsight both Jean and I agree that this show was the most stressful event we have ever entered, neither one of us wanting to admit to the other that we were not confident. Lisa duly showed better than we expected and received a well deserved second place in a large class, post graduate, awarded by Nancy Holland of the famous Sonderwald affix. It had been a hard long slog, and we knew it wasn't over just yet. It took us another six months, during which time Lisa was always in the first three at all her championships shows. Then she really bloomed. At The Dachshund Club's Championship Show in London she was awarded a Reserve CC by Mrs Cole-Hamilton. Mrs Cole-Hamilton's critique read: *Sinclair's Cairnsilk Black Diamond, another quality Black-and-tan I much admire, elegant yet with a lovely depth of body and length of ribbing, nice width between forelegs, good sweep of keel and short strong loin ... Moved and showed well!*

'Moved and showed well!' What a bonus, and to have been written by such a well-known and respected judge! Jean and I were walking two feet off the ground. Little did we realise that the best was yet to come. The following Saturday at The Scottish Dachshund Club's

Cairnsilk Black Diamond (Lisa to her friends) at eight months.

Championship Show, at Dumfries, and under yet another well-known judge, Margaret Hall, Lisa won her first CC with the following critique: Sinclair's Cairnsilk Black Diamond, B/T, gorgeous little bitch, long on form, ultra feminine, lovely head and dark expressive eyes framed with long ear fringes, well filled in front and kept her excellent outline on the move and went with style and drive.

This was fantastic, but the feeling of joy we felt on knowing that our perseverance with little Lisa had paid dividends was not just for the winning, but for the knowledge that we could so easily have given up. Lisa still has time to gain her next two CCs.

So the moral of this story is: If at first you don't succeed, try, try, and try again.

Our first championship show
Betty Cole-Hamilton

At Cardiff in the 1950s, my husband Dick and I each took a bitch puppy into the same class at our very first Championship Show. My own rather dull one coped okay, but Dick's, the last to be seen in a largish class, tabled well but then refused to move an inch through the roughly-cut grass, which contained her pet aversion - thistles. Nothing would budge her. Husband became more and more hot and embarrassed while Carrie, perfectly composed, one foot uplifted, eyes heavenward, remained totally immobile – impasse!

Eventually, while the rest of us waited more or less patiently, the judge (the late Lord Northesk) sent for some trestle-table tops, which were solemnly laid end to end on the offending grass. Carrie, pleased at having made her point, sailed up and down them effortlessly, after which the judge waved her vaguely in the direction of the exit. Dick, by now totally mortified and accepting dismissal as a merciful release, tucked Carrie under his arm and fled from the ring. At this he was hotly pursued by the stewards and shooed back by friendly onlookers, to be placed at the top of the line and awarded our first championship show first!

For some reason, he never persevered with his promising career as a dog handler...

11 Judging

There are three main sections in this chapter. The first two are articles about judging by eminent judges. Although these articles overlap in subject matter, it was felt worthwhile to include both of them. The first, by all-rounder Terry Thorn, describes in some detail the steps involved in a career in judging. The second, by breed specialist Dr Sylvia Kershaw, is concerned with ring etiquette and the actual judging, and is reproduced with the kind permission of the Dachshund Club, together with the humorous, but oh-so-telling, cartoon by Sheila E Dolan, reproduced on page 161. The third section, by yet another eminent judge, Robert Cole, includes line drawings of six Dachshunds and invites you, the reader, to use your own judgement in placing them.

Ch/Ir Ch Shardagang Masterplan at Bothlyn: a Wire beautifully prepared for the ring, owned by Elizabeth Fulton. Photo: David Dalton

To become a judge
Terry Thorn

Judging dogs, like judging any animal, is an art form. I firmly believe that a person is born with these talents. No matter how much effort one puts into the study of anatomy or individual breed points, the acquired knowledge does not always filter through until it comes to practice. Many people know the points of dogs inside out and are considered well-informed authorities on their own breeds but, unfortunately, this pure sense of knowledge cannot always be delivered either orally or in written form when they are faced with a class of dogs to be placed in the correct order of judging.

To those who consider they have the desired attributes I give this strong advice: *Don't run before you can walk.* The ladder you climb before becoming a recognised judge has many rungs, and these may only be taken one at a time. To be successful you must adhere to a strict order of requirements and achievements, because any short-cuts may well be disadvantageous later on in your career. It is essential to *play the game* fairly and squarely.

Are you ready to judge?

For instance, no-one can hope to become a judge of any real standing without first establishing some credibility as a successful breeder and exhibitor. It is vital to establish respect from your fellow exhibitors and from judges. If you breed inferior or mediocre stock and achieve little success in the show ring, why then should your fellow exhibitors have faith in your ability to judge dogs that are of far better quality than anything you have produced?

When established as both a breeder and exhibitor of quality stock, then, and only then, should you accept your first judging appointment. As we are talking about Dachshunds, I have to say that I consider it quite impertinent for people to accept an invitation to judge any variety other than their own as a first assignment. For example, if you specialise in Miniature Long-haired Dachshunds, what right do you have to start your judging career with Wires or Smooths? Unfortunately, nowadays this appears to be the 'norm', and it is a common occurrence for 'first-timers' to accept all six varieties at Open Shows. No wonder entries for these events suffer!

Progress up the ladder depends greatly on how your peers rate your ability in the ring. You would be foolish to expect recommendations for further appointments if you made a complete mess of your first endeavour, either by failing to interpret The Kennel Club Breed Standard or by ignorance of basic ring procedure. On the latter point I would suggest that aspiring judges read the Kennel Club's *Guide to Judges* and watch top all-rounder judges in action to learn about efficiency when making decisions.

To make further advancement in a career in judging you must bide your time. A person who commands respect, after being discussed by breed club committees, will be placed on one of the judging lists, thereby gaining the first important endorsement that he or she is 'on the way'.

There are usually three or four judging lists for each breed or variety, depending on its numerical size. The Kennel Club requirement is for a minimum of three lists: A1, A2, and B. These lists, updated each year by all breed clubs, have to be submitted to The Kennel Club with the other annual returns. Also to be included with the annual returns to The Kennel Club is a statement of the Club's criteria for inclusion on the various lists.

- The A1 list must include judges who award Challenge Certificates (CCs) and are endorsed by club support.
- The A2 list is for judges who also have the club's support and have judged enough classes and dogs to be ready to award CCs. A usual requirement for inclusion is for the person to have judged at least one club show plus a number of other shows.

- The B list is usually for judges who have breed club support to judge at open, limit, or championship shows at which there are no CCs on offer.
- Some numerically high breeds, such as Golden Retrievers or Cavalier King Charles Spaniels, have C lists for judges on the very first rung of the ladder.

Other breeds

Word of mouth reports about your judging ability can result in invitations to judge breeds other than your own. In Dachshunds, this would mean other varieties within the breed and, as there are no closely allied breeds, other hounds of various shapes and sizes.

Do not accept appointments just to boost your ego. Judging breeds other than your own must be taken very seriously. Seminars and lectures should be attended and hands-on experience should be gained. Many people who have the well-being of their own breed at heart will be only too willing to impart their knowledge to aspiring judges and consider it most important that you start off with a proper grounding.

In all cases, it is best to purchase the relevant Kennel Club Breed Standard, obtainable direct from The Kennel Club. Each standard comes in a loose leaf form and, for a very reasonable sum, one group at a time can be bought. Books on the breed written by experts should be purchased and studied carefully. This, combined with hands-on practice and tuition, will start you off on the right foot.

Ch Pipersvale Chocolat Royale, owned by Betty Munt.

It is an essential part of Kennel Club requirements that you keep and maintain detailed records of all your judging. Whether by means of index card system, books, or computer, you must back up these details by retaining all catalogues and judging books in case written verification of your written record is required at a later date.

Image and profile

If you judge well and are considered by most to be efficient, friendly and kind to the dogs you handle, then you will gradually build up an image. The more you judge, the more you will be asked to judge, and your profile in the world of show dogs will grow.

After officiating at your first open or limit show, and hopefully following this by a succession of more such shows, including one, two or even three breed club events, you will be considered 'ripe' for awarding Kennel Club CCs. This would normally be for your own breed, with which you have enjoyed most success and gained most judging experience. In the case of Dachshunds it would be for your own particular variety. After receiving your first invitation to award CCs you will be sent a Kennel Club questionnaire, which must be completed fully and accurately down to the last point. It must then be returned to the society inviting you, where it will be scrutinised by committee members. If it is considered to be worthy of submission to The Kennel Club it will be forwarded by the secretary of the society inviting you.

Before putting the questionnaire before the Judges Sub-Committee, The Kennel Club Judges Department usually writes to other breed clubs within the relevant breed, asking whether their committees consider the candidate ready to award CCs. The clubs are all sent a copy of the list of completed judging appointments submitted by the candidate, to help them form a rational opinion. After a set deadline for replies, The Kennel Club Judges Sub-Committee will form an opinion and the recommendation for approval or non-approval will be passed on to The Kennel Club General Committee for final decision.

If you are approved you will be informed by the secretary of the nominating society. You have now stepped up to the second rung of the ladder and completed a major hurdle in your judging career. Should you wish to pursue your career further and expand into other breeds, this will need a great deal of patience and learning. This can only be achieved by considerable study and attending many seminars and breed lectures. You will also have to attend a great many shows as a spectator to watch carefully the breed or breeds in which you are interested.

Method

Before embarking on a judging career I consider it most important to study the methods and ring procedures of the top judges. Without being intentionally hurtful to breed specialists, I would strongly advise you to watch the top all-rounders in action. They are the professionals and have got where they are because of their knowledge and efficiency.

Ultimately, all judges adopt the method most suited to them. It can be adjusted and finely tuned along the way, but in general should be used without deviation, no matter what breed they are judging.

For the uninitiated I will begin with the very first appointment. Usually, after about five to seven years from the start of your exhibiting and breeding, and providing you have been successful, you will receive an invitation to judge. This is usually by letter. If you reply in the affirmative and accept the appointment, the secretary of the inviting society will reply on behalf of the committee confirming the engagement and the agreed terms. These three letters then form a binding judging contract.

Shortly before the show you should receive a marked schedule giving details of your entry, together with your show pass, car park label and letter informing you what time you will be required to be at the show.

Usually it is best to arrive at the venue at least half an hour before your scheduled time of judging. Report to the Secretary, who will furnish you with your judging book and point you in the direction of the judges' reception area, where you will be given a welcoming hot drink. This reception area is often shared by the ring stewards, a band of loyal supporters who form a most important and integral part of every show. Try to meet your allocated steward and introduce yourself. Get onto first-name terms if possible. All stewards are very friendly and helpful people and will put you completely at ease on your first big day. You will find that many stewards are themselves aspiring judges and officiate not only to help but to gain more knowledge of the breeds for which they steward.

Arrive at the ringside at least five or six minutes before you are due to start judging. Make sure the table is firm and not at all rocky. If you are to judge a table dog such as a Dachshund you must decide at which end you would like the mat. Never let the dog face the sun. If you are judging Miniature Dachshunds ensure that the scales are in place on the table, together with the 5kg (11lb) weights, remembering that it is forbidden by Kennel Club regulations to judge these varieties without first weighing each exhibit at the start of the class.

If your steward has not already done so, take a quick walk around the ring to make sure there are no foreign objects on the ground that could injure the dogs' feet. Inform the steward where you require him or her to stand your new dogs and clarify where you would like to stand the dogs with repeat entries. Explain to the steward where you will be placing your winners and remember that these must be from left to right in order of descendancy: first down to VHC (Very Highly Commended). They must be placed in the centre of the ring.

Now you are ready to begin and your first class will enter the ring. The exhibitors will stand their dogs sideways on in show pose. You should walk once up and down, at the same time having a quick glance at the heads, fronts, quarters and hocks. Unless you have a particularly large class or a small ring it is best to send the dogs once around the ring to enable you to compare side gait and note how they carry their heads and tails in relation to the carriage requirements listed in the breed standard, When the dogs have completed their pacing around the ring, the first dog should be placed on the table. Obviously, with all Dachshunds and other table dogs this would be on the table with the head facing you.

Make a thorough examination of the dog, without being heavy-handed. Check the teeth and bite at the same time. Provided that the ring is big enough, it is best to move the dogs in a triangle. This enables you to see the dog coming, going and in side gait once again. Go through the whole class in exactly the same way. When all the dogs have been examined and moved, they should all be back in their original line and standing in a show stance.

The dogs are ready now for your final assessment and placing. Be positive in your selections. Although at first it might take longer, your ultimate aim should be to judge each dog in your entry in one to two minutes. If you can achieve this as your norm it will prove your efficiency as a judge (providing of course that you come up with the correct results as well!)

Concentration

The main failing of unsuccessful and bad judges is lack of concentration. It is fatal to lose concentration during judging, even for a minute. It of the utmost importance that your mind never wanders from the job in hand. So very often we see judges, after giving the dogs the necessary examination, wandering aimlessly up and down the line of exhibits looking completely lost. They move all the dogs for a second and sometimes even a third time. Then

Hobbithill Belthil (Standard Smooth), standing without a lead. Photo: Lionel Young

they go through the motions of feeling parts of the body again. It is my contention that, if the judge has been concentrating right from the start of the class, he or she should remember all the virtues and failings of each dog. The judge should then be able to place each dog in order of merit in a quick and efficient manner.

With full concentration there should never be a need to 'go over' an exhibit twice and only on rare occasions should the dog be asked to move across the ring and back a second or third time.

At the conclusion of the class and when the dogs have been placed, the steward should be instructed to request the winner to remain in the ring for you, the judge, to make a written critique on the merits and failings of the dog. You will already have marked your winners down in your judging book and you will find space provided in the book for written comments. Written comments are of vital importance in the world of dog showing and they give a good demonstration of the judge's knowledge of the breed. The two very popular weekly canine papers, *Dog World* and *Our Dogs*, provide stamped, addressed envelopes for every judge, and these critiques and class awards are usually published within a month of the show being held. Most exhibitors consider written critiques as part and parcel of the judging contract and take a dim view of judges who fail to produce the goods!

Good luck with your judging, and remember that the whole purpose of dog shows is to further the cause, to produce the 'perfect' dog in each breed. Judging is a serious business, but can be pure delight for those who participate.

Judging

Dr Sylvia Kershaw

It is commonly said by the ignorant that you will never reach the stage of making up champions until you are a judge! This is false. There are so many successful exhibitors who have either judged very little or not at all that this view is not worth considering.

The good judge

Out of every club's judging list, probably less than half are really good judges. Obviously, everyone who undertakes judging thinks they are good at it, or desires to be good at it, so we can consider the factors that make good judging. First of all there is a basic personality that may ultimately make a good judge. That is not to say for a moment that those personalities who will do so are any nicer or more attractive than those who judge badly. Possibly the opposite is true: that those personalities we admire and like may make poor judges! Gentleness, kindness, the desire to please, consideration for other people's feelings and warm friendships among exhibitors are definite handicaps for good judges. Above all, those who find it difficult to make decisions and are not prepared to make mistakes and be criticised for it should not put themselves forward.

So what basic personalities are most likely to succeed? First of all I would place those with a keen observation of detail and a good memory for dogs, ability to make decisions quickly and stick to them, strength of purpose, and sufficient humility not to be upset by the criticism that will follow. Remember, only one owner will normally be satisfied with a judge; all the rest will feel their precious dog has been slighted!

Of course, many other factors are necessary, and first of all is a real knowledge of the breed. This may take years to acquire, and certainly needs long observation of the breed or breeds at various stages of their development. It also requires frequent watching of dogs of that breed in the show ring and trying to understand what the judge on the day is doing and the reasons behind the placing. Some people with a keen observation and some knowledge of the breed can learn quickly, but most progres much more slowly.

There are some 'all-rounders' with no personal knowledge of Dachshunds who make a very good job of judging the breed, but they are few and far between – and getting fewer. The main reason for this is that many all-rounders nowadays have a superficial knowledge of a number of breeds rather than the real depth of knowledge of dogs in general that some of the past judges had.

There is no doubt in my mind that sitting round a judging ring enjoying the latest gossip with the other visitors will not give you enough knowledge and experience of the breed to make you a good judge. Concentration is necessary, together with a fundamental interest in the actual dogs (not owners) and an ability to observe and assess the actual virtues and faults on show. My own feeling is that no passing of examinations, which can be completed by any moderately intelligent person in a year or two, can compare with years of really concentrated watching, observing and consideration.

Added to this there must be mental honesty, by which I mean the kind of honesty which satisfies you as well as that which is apparent to others. No consideration must be given to anything or anyone other than the actual dogs in the ring. The owners or handlers are unimportant and can be ignored. This can work both ways. There may be those handling dogs in the ring that you really do not like, there may be those you like very much, or there may be someone who arouses your sympathy for some reason. None of these matters should have any influence on your judging, except that you may give extra help to the inexperienced in showing their dogs. The worst kind of judging arises from those who, with an eye to future judging appointments, favour the dogs of people who may be thought to have influence. Such 'judges' have no love of the breed, only of themselves, and the breed suffers from their placings. Even experienced judges may think to themselves, 'Oh, that's Mrs So-and-So, she is well-known and has lovely dogs, I must pay special attention to her dog.' This is not true and honest judging. Well-known breeders and exhibitors can produce poor dogs – only the dogs in the ring on the day matter.

On the move

In addition to studying The Kennel Club Breed Standard and Sayer's *Illustrated Standard*, and knowing the anatomy of the dog in a standing position, perhaps the most important and difficult aspect is to judge dogs moving. It is my experience that very few judges can really assess correct movement in the Dachshund, resulting in some really poor judging

The Standard is quite clear: *Movement should be free and flowing. Stride should be long with the drive coming from the hindquarters when viewed from the side. Viewed from in front or behind the legs and feet should move parallel to each other with the distance apart being the width of the shoulder and hip joints respectively.*

Note the first part of this: *... free and flowing. Stride should be long with drive coming from hindquarters.* This is where so many judges fall down. They can quite easily see whether the hind legs are parallel to one another but to see whether there is *drive* and give credit for a long flowing stride seems beyond them. Naturally the outline of the moving dog must remain the same as the standing dog, being carried forward smoothly. The forelegs must not be thrown too high in a jerky movement, nor must the hind legs patter along under the body. The hocks must be flexed (bent) and extended behind the root of the tail so that they are driving the body forward.

It takes an expert to describe correct movement in words; generally, it has to be looked for in the ring and, when found, watched again and again and valued highly. It means that the dog is made right and can do the job for which it was originally intended. (See *Dog Steps* book and video by Rachel Page Elliot). It may be difficult to assess movement indoors in a small ring, particularly in Standards who require a really large ring and a good surface. Many indoor rings only give enough space for two or three strides along the side of the ring, especially if the exhibits are good movers with a really long stride. In such cases the judge should state in a critique that it was impossible to assess movement, and that their placings might have been different if movement could have been taken into account.

The critique

This brings us to the critique, which every judge should write and publish after judging, Today there are judges who do not write critiques. I believe there are three reasons for this: arrogance, ignorance and laziness. The arrogant ones are usually experienced judges who say to themselves: 'Well, they came for my opinion and I have given it. They should not expect anything more from me with all my knowledge and experience.' The ignorant are afraid to write anything down in case it exposes their ignorance. The lazy ones just cannot be bothered. I would say to the last group that it is the busiest people who seem to find time to write critiques for the sake of the breed.

Not every judge is a fluent writer, but the main value of the critique is that it explains why the judge made the final decision: why one dog was put above or below another. Provided the criticism is not harsh or unkind, this is what readers want to know, and what will help breeders take a step forward. On the Continent, every dog in the ring has to be evaluated and a critique on each has to be given to the owner. Surely it is not too much to comment on two dogs in each class, which is all the dog press have room for. Incidentally, I have noticed some judges now are only giving the first two dogs' names in each class; the third surely should be mentioned, at least by name.

Controlling the ring

The other important factor in judging is to be able to 'control' the ring. This means that the judge must have sound and up-to-date knowledge of Kennel Club rules and be aware at all times of what is going on in the ring. A good steward is an enormous help but, with a poor steward, the judge must be prepared to do the whole thing. Checking to see that the entries in the class are all there and that the handlers are wearing the correct numbers is the steward's job but, if it is not done correctly, the judge can end up in a terrible muddle. The usual routine is for the dogs in the class to be moved around the ring once, twice or three times, according to the judge's preference.

Examining the dogs

The judge then examines each dog on the table. Now the dog should stand quietly in show stance, and nothing is gained by pulling the dog about; rough handling of Dachshunds at this stage can make a dog hate shows for life. The matters that can be assessed on the table are the head, eye colour and shape, ear set, mouth (teeth), ribbing, angle of shoulder, feet and tail. None of these require a lot of handling and, when I see judges repeatedly running hands over the dog, pushing here and pulling there, I understand that they do not really know what they are looking for. All the rest of the points required are better assessed on the floor, and particularly in movement.

Moving the dogs

After the table examination each dog should be moved separately, generally away from the judge and towards the judge, sometimes in a triangle. The use of a triangle depends to some extent on the size of the ring. If it is a nice large ring the best view of movement from the side is watching the dogs go round the ring, but in a smaller ring it may be necessary to see each dog from the side separately.

When each dog has been seen separately they can be moved again right round the ring, either altogether or separately, as many times as the judge wishes. When they come to a standstill and are posed for a few moments, the judge can select the first five, placing them in order in the centre of the ring, the first on the judge's left and so on.

The final selection
Be quite definite about the placings; handlers can get confused about the order, and there are

The Champion as only Three Judges Saw Her, by Sheila E Dolan.

a few 'pushers' who will try to get in at a higher place. This is where a good memory for dogs comes in: sometimes the handler may change, but the judge should remember the dog, not the handler. Now the judge marks the judging book and makes any notes required for a critique on the first two in the class.

Judging further classes

The next class is judged in the same way, but there may be a further complication. In Britain (but not usually elsewhere in the world) a dog may be entered in several classes: for instance Puppy, Novice and Junior. It is the steward's job to organise the dogs already seen by the judge in a previous class at the side of the ring and place them in order according to their previous awards. When the judge has completed judging the new dogs in the class the steward should call the judge's attention to the dogs that have already been seen, and remind the judge of their previous placings. A poor steward may overlook this and it is important that the judge remembers how the dogs were placed previously. I have seen judges get in a muddle over this and end up placing the dogs in different order from that of the class judged only 20 minutes ago! This shows a lack of concentration on the judge's part and can upset exhibitors considerably, doing the judge's reputation considerable harm. The judge should be in full control of the ring and both the people and dogs in it, at all times, and this requires complete concentration.

When all the classes have been judged the winners of each class are brought into the ring for the judging of Best of Sex. The same procedure takes place except that, as the judge has already seen them on the table, it is not necessary to repeat that. At an Open Show in Great Britain, where dogs and bitches are shown together in a class, the final winner will be Best of Breed. At Championship shows the best dog and the best bitch will compete for Best of Breed.

In conclusion...

Anyone judging for the first time will find all this difficult to achieve, especially if they have an unhelpful steward. However, it is advisable to start at the smaller shows, where the classes are smaller and there is time to get used to the atmosphere. Any experienced exhibitor who has observed what is going on in the ring, not just vaguely watched it, will have no problems.

It is likely that, to be invited to judge, an exhibitor will have shown consistently good stock (not necessarily champions) over a number of years. One top animal is not enough, as it could just be luck; there must be a succession of dogs of good type. This takes some doing but, in the end, a good breeder will be asked to judge.

My final advice is not to dither when judging. The longer you take (within limits), the more likely you are to make mistakes. Be decisive; make up your mind. Even if you are wrong, it is not the end of the world, and exhibitors will not thank you for keeping them long after the rest of the show has finished. They will remember and not wish to show under you again. Be honest, be decisive, make use of real knowledge and understanding of the breed, and above all, concentrate on the matter in hand, and you will make a successful judge. Take as your motto that, in dog judging, it is only the dogs that matter

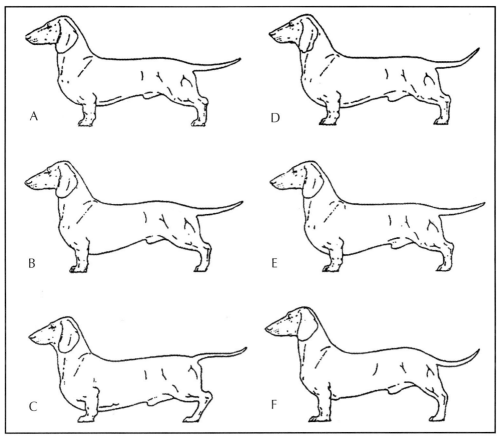

'You be the judge'
Robert Cole

With maximum discussion based on comparative decisions, I have selected six Standard Smooth-haired Dachshunds, each contributing in profile a variety of virtues and faults, some serious, some superficial. These are represented in the drawing above. Between the six almost every physical breed characteristic one might encounter in showing is represented.

You be the judge – of the six, which would you place first, second, third, fourth, fifth and sixth, and why?

First

First place goes to **Dachshund E**. This is the illustrated approach to the ideal I formulated in 1983 as an interpretation of optimum proportions. Care at that time was taken to include and make obvious those characteristics deemed important by breeders, such as the head. The skull is only slightly arched; the less stop the better (pronounced bridge bones over the eyes should not be confused with the stop); the muzzle is slightly arched; the skull and muzzle tapered toward the nose. The ears are set near the top of the head and of the correct length, not pointed or folded. The size of the head is in balance with the body.

This example is correctly low to ground, short-legged and long-bodied.

For those more familiar with less unorthodox breeds, this excerpt complemented by my drawing still requires elaboration. It helps to be aware that, unlike in orthodox breeds where it is level with the bottom of the chest, the Dachshund's elbow positions well above the bottom of the chest. The foreleg is short, but the Dachshund is also low to the ground because its body is brought down between the elbows and rests over the curved inner surface of the upper arms.

Describing part of the Dachshund's forelegs in profile with emphasis on the above-the-bottom-of-the-brisket position of the elbow increases appreciation, but it is the shape of the front leg viewed head-on where there is most confusion. Correct interpretation is easier understood when depicted rather than described.

The foreleg of the illustrated approach to ideal shown head-on is straight not from the elbow down, as in most breeds, but (because of the high position of the elbow) only from the wrist down. The forearm between the wrist and the elbow curves around the body.

Second

A sound dog, Dachshund A lacks depth of body, which in all likelihood will come with maturity. Even if depth never fully comes, this Dachshund is very sound, with excellent proportions.

Perhaps because of immaturity, the arch over the loin is slightly more pronounced than in the first placed dog but, where the back should be level, between the withers and the arch, the topline is all it should be. The good tail set is a continuation of the spine above sound hindquarters. This dog is sound in front, the slight slope to the pastern bringing support directly under its forequarters.

Third

Third place goes to Dachshund D. Structurally, this example resembles the first place dog, with the exception of four minor faults.
- The ears are folded, a minor fault that often goes unnoticed.
- The short head is more noticeable and serious.
- The dog has a dewlap.
- There is a kink in the tail.

Fourth

Dachshund B has many good points to offset its obvious faults. Virtue of head, neck, body, shoulders, bone, pelvis and feet are some. Four obvious faults are:
- a short upper arm
- no slope to pastern
- over-long rib-cage
- lowset ears (a minor fault)

A short upper arm, which brings the elbows forward on the body, reducing the fore-chest and straightening the pastern (making it vertical), is not uncommon. The long body (rib-cage, not loin) changes the length-to-height ratio. The front leg in conjunction with this vertical pastern often lacks typical curve in forearm. The front leg, head on, is often straight and, because there is no necessity for the feet to incline slightly outwards to obtain maximum static support, this incorrect Dachshund assembly often has appeal. It is unlikely this dog will ever receive consideration for CCs.

Fifth

Not worthy of CC consideration. Dachshund F exhibits a number of serious and minor faults.

- The head has a stop: in a Dachshund, the less pronounced the stop the more typical the Dachshund.
- The ears are high.
- The shoulders are steep, causing a dip in the topline.
- The upper arm is steep (notice the low and forward position of the elbow).
- The front pastern is vertical.
- The feet constitute a departure from the required low-to-ground appearance.
- The breast-bone is too low (in relation to withers and brisket) and, carried down, ends too abruptly under the body.
- The loin is long.
- The pelvis is steep, magnifying the dip in topline and causing a reduction in hindquarter angulation at stifle and hock, raising the rear and lowering the tail set

Sixth

Not worthy of CC consideration. Dachshund C has a very nice head (less dewlap) but, because of departure elsewhere, the head does not balance with the body.

- The most obvious departure is too much body depth. The body from shoulder to brisket should, in my opinion, be one head length deep. This Dachshund's body is deeper through than optimum, appearing clumsy and incapable of work.
- This example is steep in the shoulder, but manages to retain a degree of fore-chest because the elbow has not been forced forward on the body, as usually happens when the shoulders are steep. Instead, the body has been forced down between faulty elbows by steep shoulders. This forces the upper arm (humerus) to adopt a horizontal position, and positions the elbow too high on the body.
- This dog lacks the required tuck-up and has a flat and perhaps short pelvis. Unlike some breeds, where this high tailset would cause the tail to flag, it is often only at the base of the tail that this departure is noticeable.
- An over-long rear pastern causes this dog to adopt a sickle-hock position to bring support more under the rear end, a problem not uncommon among short-legged, low-to-the-ground breeds.

One more fault...

Another serious fault, not exhibited among these six, is knuckling over (faulty structure of the wrist joint, allowing it to double forward under the weight of the dog). The example most susceptible to knuckling over would be Dachshund F.

12 Conformation and movement

Robert Cole

This chapter was written by Robert Cole for The Dachshund Club and is reproduced here with the club's generous permission, along with copies of his line drawings, which are as relevant and valuable today as when they were first produced.

Proportions

Ideal proportions do not receive mention in the Dachshund Standard. Lawrence Alder Horswell, noted American Dachshund authority, attempted to define ideal Dachshund proportions in the 1960s. I adopted four of his proportional suggestions when I produced my own illustrated ideal, which in the end bears little resemblance to Horswell's copyrighted diagram. I adopted his suggestion that *head length equals length of neck, length of tail and depth of body*. I did not agree with his contention that *the back is two head-lengths, the body - breastbone to hock in show pose - three head-lengths*. Nor did I agree with his illustrated shoulder lay-back, breastbone position, slope to front pastern or angulation at hock. Be that as it may, it was Lawrence Alden Horswell's *Diagram of the Dachshund in Show Pose* that influenced my *Illustrated Interpretation of the Dachshund Standard* (see page 121).

Conformation and movement

The ideal (fig 12.1) is twice as long from breastbone to buttocks as it is at the withers. Although it differs in a number of respects from The Dachshund Club official illustrated ideal by J P Sayer (1967), the ratio of 2:1 is the same as the British illustrated ideal. If it is 2.5cm (1in) less in length (fig 12.2) the body in proportion to height is too short; if it is 2.5 cm more in length (fig 12.3) the body is too long. Extreme body length departures such as these seldom occur. There is more likelihood that forequarter structure will alter length to height ratio; an aspect that will be dealt with later in detail.

Depth of body (the distance from withers to the deepest part of the bottom of the chest) is an important proportion for appearance and function. I agree with those official Dachshund ideals which depict the depth of body as equal to length of head (American Standard). A body slightly deeper than one head length (fig 12.4) appears too heavy in proportion to the other parts. This could happen but it is more likely that the extra depth will occur at the bottom of the chest (fig 12.5), reducing ground clearance. Either way – awkward or cramped – more than ample is undesirable. However, too low a chest does not necessarily mean the body has too much depth – the cause may lie elsewhere.

Length of forearm is a major consideration because length of leg can affect proportional balance drastically. The Standard is vague, requiring only that the forearm be short in comparison to other breeds. But how short is short? Well, length of foreleg in dogs has traditionally been related to depth of body. A *long* leg is longer than depth of body (Basenji). A moderate leg is as long as the body is deep (Boxer). A *short* leg is shorter than body depth (Beagle). It follows that a Dachshund's foreleg is shorter than *short*.

The Beagle's foreleg from elbow to ground is approximately four-fifths its depth of body. Its elbow are level with bottom of the chest. To demonstrate exactly how short the Dachshund's foreleg is compared to the Beagle's (fig 12.6a – overleaf), I have graphically raised the illustrated ideal's body until the bottom of the chest is level with the elbow (fig 12.6b – overleaf). In this extreme departure from type the foreleg can be seen to be proportionally shorter than the Beagle's. Seen level with the bottom of the chest, the measurement from elbow to ground is three-fifths the depth of the body: one fifth less than the Beagle's.

The Dachshund is not low to ground just because its legs are short. It is low to ground because, in conjunction with a short leg, its body is deep and the chest drops down well below the elbow. A foreleg longer than the ideal three-fifths of the body depth raises the body (fig 12.7 – overleaf)

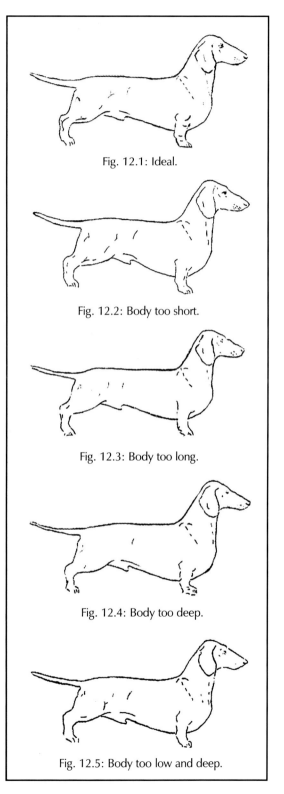

Fig. 12.1: Ideal.

Fig. 12.2: Body too short.

Fig. 12.3: Body too long.

Fig. 12.4: Body too deep.

Fig. 12.5: Body too low and deep.

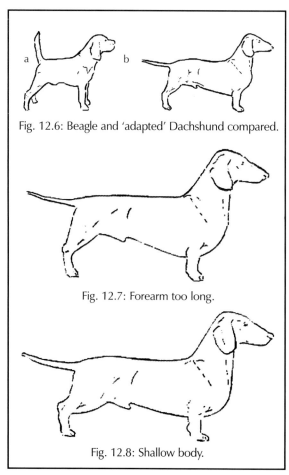

Fig. 12.6: Beagle and 'adapted' Dachshund compared.

Fig. 12.7: Forearm too long.

Fig. 12.8: Shallow body.

and slightly changes the height to length ratio. This example differs from the illustrated ideal in that its forearm (the portion of the foreleg between the elbow and the wrist) is too long.

The foreleg can *appear* too long when the body is shallow (fig 12.8). The body should be as deep as the head, neck and tail are long.

When the body is shallow the ratio of height to length does not change unless the forequarters are faulty. Faulty forequarters present an entirely different picture.

The front end

The Dachshund's shoulder blade, and the angle at which it is laid back, is a primary consideration when we are considering the front end, and a good place to start. To begin with, it should lay back at an *oblique* angle. Some writers advise that this is the best way to describe the angle. Others claim that the ideal shoulder blade angle for the Dachshund is 45°. Still others claim that 45° is impossible for a dog.

Aware that shoulder blade angulation can be a controversial subject, I was careful to include a broken line to represent the bony ridge running up the centre of the shoulder blade (fig 12.9) when I drew an ideal Dachshund in outline (fig 12.1).

This ridge, or *spine* as it is called, can be felt with the fingertips and is the most precise way of determining the angle of the shoulder blade. I drew this ridge at an oblique angle of 50° off the horizontal. However, another method of measuring shoulder lay-back is used more often, and by this method the same shoulder blade measures 45°. I was careful, when I drew an ideal Dachshund front skeleton (fig 12.9), not to combine these two methods of measuring shoulder lay-back as many artists do, and as I have done in the past.

The two methods of measuring shoulder blade lay-back are illustrated in fig 12.10. A line from point A (commonly called the point of the shoulder) to the top of the blade (point B) produces an angle, represented by a broken line, of 45°. These points can be felt with the fingertips, and this method of measuring is fast and convenient. A more precise measurement can be made, along the spine of the shoulder blade, from point C to point B.

Less oblique, this method produces an angle of 50° off the horizontal.

In the April 1979 issue of the *American Kennel Gazette*, Curtis M Brown (author of *The Art and Science of Judging Dogs*) reported that there could be as much as 9° difference in the two methods of measuring shoulder lay-back. He was of the opinion that, before a breed be allowed to change its Standard to require a 45° lay-back, the measurement method should be specified, and the responsible club should be required to make actual measurements on a large number of good representatives to determine what angle actually existed in the population.

Artists are responsible for the general unawareness that there are two ways of measuring shoulder lay-back. They do as McDowell Lyon did in his book *The Dog in Action* and as I have done in fig 12.11, rearranging the bone structure so that, as in the horse, the spine of shoulder blade lines up with the point of the shoulder (upper arm), both methods producing the same 45° result.

Fronts

There has always been a degree of controversy over how straight the Dachshund's front legs, viewed head on, should be. The Dachshund Standards describe the shape of the front legs viewed head-on as *not appearing absolutely straight*. This correct but less-than-

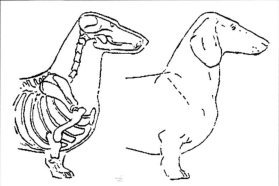

Fig 12.9: The ideal shoulder blade.

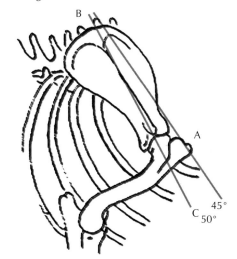

Fig 12.10: Two methods of measuring shoulder lay-back.

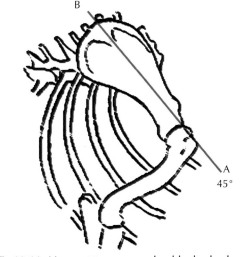

Fig 12.11: How *not* to measure shoulder lay-back.

comprehensive description has been paraphrased at various times here and abroad by breeders and authors as: *partly straight, straight but not in one straight column* and *perfectly straight*. If required to paraphrase the description in the Standard in less than half a dozen words, I would word it *straight from the chest down*. However, as a multi-breed judge, I know that this description will be subject to misinterpretation, especially outside the breed.

To those familiar with the Dachshund's unique forequarter assembly, *straight from the chest down* conveys a beautifully balanced mental picture. To those more familiar with highstanding or short- but straight-legged breeds, the picture may be entirely different, because they think of the elbow and the bottom of the chest as being on the same level. In the case of the Dachshund, these two features are not on the same level, which is why I began this section with an ideal (fig 12.1) posed in profile.

In profile, the Dachshunds's elbow ideally is positioned well above the bottom of the chest and well back of the forechest. The Dachshund is not only short-legged; it is also so low-slung that its foreleg is straight, viewed head-on, but only from the chest down, not from the elbow down. This kind of forequarter assembly is best described when complemented by a front view drawing of the illustrated ideal (fig 12.12). This helps to clarify what I mean by *straight from the chest down*. The foreleg is not straight from the elbow downwards, as it is in the case of higher stationed or short-but-straight-legged breeds, where the elbow is level with the bottom of the chest; it is straight from the wrist joint down. The wrist joint, not the elbow, is almost level with the bottom of the chest. Viewed from the front, the wrist joint is sometimes mistaken for elbow. At least one artist has omitted to include the pastern on this kind of front, to position the elbow level with the bottom of a low-slung chest.

Fig. 12.12: The ideal, viewed from the front.

The pastern, being the portion of the foreleg between wrist joint and pad, is the only part of the Dachshund's front leg which is straight. The forearm is not straight because the elbow is positioned close to the body, above the bottom of the chest, and must curve or wrap around the body to bring the assembly into a static (and dynamic) balance. This, as the Standard requires, brings the wrists *closer together than the shoulder joints*. This could easily have read: *elbow joints*.

Not all Dachshund authors are in accord with my view. One author has gone as far as to state: *The perfectly straight front is now preferred by most judges and it cannot be held to be incorrect.* It may well mean that this author means the pastern from wrist down is

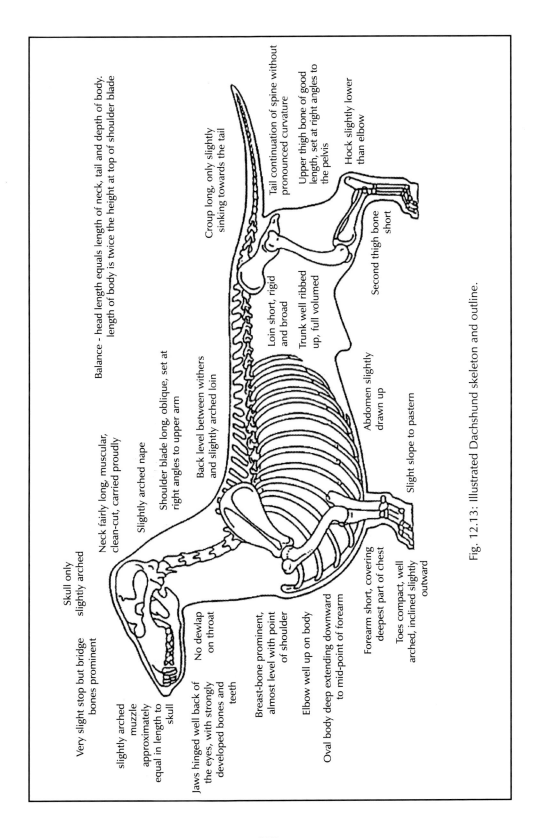

Fig. 12.13: Illustrated Dachshund skeleton and outline.

perfectly straight - not the whole foreleg. Be that as it may, there has always been a degree of controversy over how straight the Dachshund's front legs should be, either because the unique assembly is not understood, and therefore not described correctly, or because the description is incomplete.

It was because of front-end controversy (not altogether a bad thing) that this last illustration was preceded by more than a dozen drawings, each relating indirectly to the appearance of the front legs viewed head on. This resulted in an illustrated skeletal ideal (fig 12.12) and a series of proportions based on head length was eventually accepted by The American Kennel Club.

The trot

The official description of the trot can be found in the glossary of *The Book of Dogs*, official publication of the Canadian Kennel Club, and *The Complete Dog Book*, official publication of the American Kennel Club. Both glossaries describe the trot as: *A rhythmic two-beat diagonal gait in which the feet at diagonally opposite ends of the body strike the ground together*. This is as far as the official description of the trot is taken; but even though it is simple, I fail to take notice of this rule.

The official description of the trot is over simplified and I promised myself that, when I possessed the necessary specialist camera equipment, I would produce an illustrated *Dachshund Movement on the trot* update. The time has come – I have been working with a specialised motion picture camera for six years now. The drawing of a good moving Dachshund is here expanded to a real life illustrated sequence of 20 drawings. These describe a stride (one step taken by all four legs - a complete cycle). From the film footage I have taken of Dachshunds, I have selected one particular sound dog to serve as an example of typical movement on the trot in profile. Typical, not ideal, because, good as this dog is, he is not perfect. To relate this dog's structure to the way he moves, he was first filmed stacked in profile, then moved.

My illustrated sequence format (fig 12.14) always begins with the individual dog's right forearm in vertical support. Depending on the structure of the individual, the position of the three legs can vary in the first phase and, if poorly structured, can continue to position wrongly unless the dog has found some means of compensation. Having a beginning where the right front leg position is constant enables phase by phase comparisons to be made with other individuals within a breed. The complete stride took only about a third of a second, about the time it takes to say *Dachshund*.

This selected Dachshund example's action conforms to the brief description of the trot quoted at the beginning of this section. The right hind with left front diagonals strike at the same time in Phase 7, and the opposite pair of diagonals strike at the same time in Phase 17. This dog exhibits the desired two-beat gait, synchronised pairs of diagonals having contact with the ground twice during each stride. However, this brief but correct statement only describes about 10% of the action that occurs at the trot.

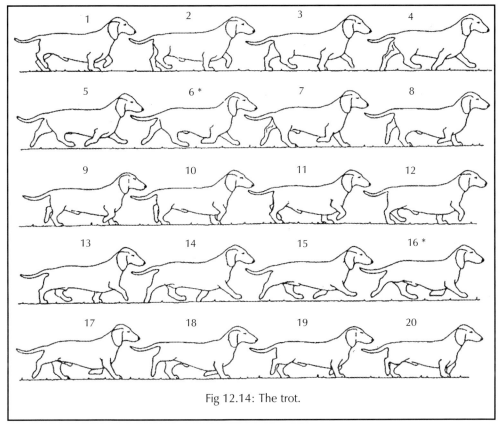

Fig 12.14: The trot.

In addition to diagonal pairs of feet striking the ground together, diagonal pairs of feet should lift off the ground at the same time. In addition to striking, feet at diagonally opposite ends of the body should relinquish support and propulsion simultaneously (Phase 4 and Phase 14). Then there is the phase that follows lift of diagonal feet, the phase I call the classic phase.

Artists traditionally only provide a single drawing to represent typical action at the trot for a specific breed of dog. The phase usually selected is where a front leg is reaching fully forward, and a hind leg is extended fully rearward. I once felt that the Dachshund, with its short legs and long, low-slung body, would be unlikely to step beyond the imprint left by the front, and therefore could not exhibit a period of suspension. Now, I have proof on film that Dachshunds do utilise a period of suspension at the trot.

The Dachshund utilises a period of suspension twice during each stride cycle, as illustrated (∗) in Phase 6 and again in Phase 16. It is during Phase 6 and Phase 16 of the stride, when the dog is unsupported, that most distance is covered. Without this period of suspension, distance covered would have to rely solely on body movement forward over supporting legs.

13 Dachshunds abroad

Australia: Dachshunds down-under

Australia is the perfect environment for the Dachshund, and what a privilege it is to be asked to judge there. Fortunately, the breed standards are the same, although ring etiquette differs slightly. We in the Old Country are always interested in news from Australia and rely heavily on people like Kath and Andy Bethel who bring back the updates.

Kath Bethel judged in New South Wales, South Australia, in 1992. Andrew Bethel also had the pleasure of judging all Dachshund classes in Newcastle, New South Wales in 1996 – and what wonderful tales they brought back to an eager audience.

Aust Ch Hampdach Dignitary.

British imports

I think United Kingdom interest in the Australian Dachshund is influenced by the Australian's foresight in importing some of Britain's best breeding stock. The Australians certainly have a canny eye for a good Dachshund. It should be remembered that all Dachshunds, from whatever country, began with imports, Germany being their country of origin.

Aust Ch Hampdach Royal Parade.

Kath and Andrew Bethel have exported some very fine Hampdach Dachshunds to Australia, such as Aust Ch Hampdach Dignitary to Mrs and Miss Neal in Queensland. Dignitary went on to sire a stunning 25 champions in three states. Then there was their very fine Hampdach Royal Parade, who went to Mr and Mrs Philps in New South Wales.

Aust Ch Rossini Sunset Sashe
(sire: Aust Ch Hampdach Dignitary).

It speaks volumes for the respect the United Kingdom has for Australians that we export so readily, without reserve or misgivings, to this country. Indeed, we bask in the reflected glory. This is well earned by the Australians, who are renowned for their astute breeding programmes. They breed wisely, making up many champions whose progeny produce multiple champions in their turn. Of all the English-speaking countries in the world, the Australians have complimented us the most by taking advantage of our excellent stock lines and, in their turn, exporting to places like the United States, Canada, New Zealand and Japan. Their eye for a good dog and the expertise they have developed over the years are certainly a credit to them. Behind many of their top dogs are such famous kennel names as Imber, Bowbank, D'Arisca, Silvea, Wendlitt, Stargang, Hobbithill, Womack and Bothlyn. Little wonder that so many British judges and enthusiasts feel so at home in Australia.

Bothlyn Magician (Jack), exported by Elizabeth Fulton to Howard and Jill Smith. Photo: Animal Pics

Fortunately for our judges, the breed standards are much the same as in the United Kingdom, although the Miniature varieties are not weighed before being shown and, interestingly, their Miniatures do not seem to have escalated in size. Rather, they seem to work on an honour system, which has done the breed no harm. In my opinion it is a far more sensible way of dealing with size and I have long been a campaigner in this country for a little extra weight being awarded to the Miniature dog in all varieties. It seems rather unfair when a dog, by the very nature of his species, is usually larger than the bitch.

The question of quarantine
When deciding to export or import, quarantine has to be considered. Here I am doubtful about agreeing with the lobbyists who want the laws relaxed. On the one hand I am aware that it is terribly hard on the dog. There again, so is rabies ... so what is the alternative? Perhaps one day someone will come up with a sensible alternative, one that will benefit both animal and human alike.

Six months is a very long time in the life of a dog but, with loving and caring owners, much can be done to lighten its isolation. I found the photographs that Elizabeth Fulton (Bothlyn Miniature Wires) lent me for this book most interesting. Elizabeth exported a very promising puppy, Bothlyn Magician, to Howard and Jill Smith in Victoria, and just two months out of quarantine they made him up to Australian champion. The future looks bright for 'Jack', as he is known at home, and we watch his progress with much interest. Jack has already sired a puppy who, as far as Jill knows, is the youngest ever champion to be made up in Australia.

The Australian quarantine laws are different from those in Great Britain, the period lasting only three months instead of six.

Quarantine for rabies is an emotive subject, one which we should consider long and hard before coming down either for or against. We know, for instance that there used to be no cure for rabies, and that it is still fatal unless treated very swiftly after exposure. Also that it is a horrifying disease that attacks the nervous system of any mammal and is passed on from the bite of an infected animal. Rabies destroys the cells of the brain in both mammal and man; the final symptoms being hydrophobia, a violent fear of water. It is also a discomforting fact that rabies, in its most severe and infectious form, is still endemic in Africa, on the American continent and in nearly the whole of Asia, and it is not by luck alone that Australia, New Zealand, Hong Kong, Britain and Japan are completely free of it. Makes you think, doesn't it? Can we afford to allow our hearts to rule our heads? As the mother and grandmother of a large family and an owner of much-loved Dachies, I don't have the perfect answer.

I can say, however, that I wish our own quarantine quarters could be more like those in Australia, and that the duration, after adequate proof of innoculation, could be cut to three months. While recognising that the animal's physical welfare in British quarantine centres is

(Above) Jack and Jill getting acquainted in quarantine and (below) Jack running free in his pen. See how much space he has!

adequate and taking into account that these centres are closely vetted by various animal welfare societies, I feel that the psychological welfare of the animal is not taken into consideration sufficiently. I believe it comes down to space and manpower. Dogs need space and, considering that quarantine costs upwards of £2000, surely we are entitled to ask if our animals, like those in Australia, are getting value for money? I think the photographs of 'Jack' in Australia, romping and running about and already forming a bond with his new owner while in quarantine, demonstrate my point. If a picture is said to speak louder than a hundred words, these photographs surely say it all.

The Dachshund in Ireland
Wendy Jackson (Hon Secretary to The Irish Dachshund Club)
With the entire human population of Ireland, North and South, amounting to less than 6,000,000 (well short of the population of London), the number of dogs in any breed is

bound to be fairly small in comparison with England, Scotland and Wales. The total number of Dachshunds registered with The Irish Kennel Club in the year ending June 1995, including imports, was 230. In the preceding eight years the highest number registered was 289, and the lowest 199. Miniature, both Long-haired and Smooth-haired, make up the majority of registrations. The Hound Group is by far the smallest, and Dachshunds make up a quarter to a third of the overall Hound total.

The Irish Kennel Club has classified Dachshunds since 1927, but the three coat varieties were not divided until 1933. Miniatures were not recognised by The Irish Kennel Club until as late as 1975, although classification for under 5kg (11lb), or 5.5kg (12lb) for Wires, was permitted for each coat from about 1948. Only in 1989 were Miniature Wire-hairs brought into line with Longs and Smooths. Prior to their recognition in 1975, Miniatures competed against Standards for Green Stars.

The Green Star system

This is a source of some confusion to those outside Ireland. It is based on the annually prepared table determined by the number of dogs and bitches shown at each of the 22 championship shows held in Ireland during the current year. The breed club championship is not included in this calculation. The more dogs or bitches shown, the higher the index, and so the greater the number of dogs actually in the ring at any one show that will be required to obtain a Major (minimum 5 points) Green Star. Where ** are indicated by the classification for the breed, it means that two Green Stars are on offer, one for dogs and one for bitches, exactly as with Challenge Certificates (CCs) in the United Kingdom.

Where it is shown in the schedule that the Green Star index for a particular breed is 8:10:11, this means that to gain a Major, or 5-Point Green Star, there will have to be eight dogs and/or ten bitches registered with the Irish Kennel Club actually present and in the ring. The third figure refers to mixed classes. If there is only one *, this means that only one Green Star is on offer and, if the required numbers of dogs and bitches are present, the Green Star will be worth 2 points. Less or more dogs determine the number of points awarded with a minimum of one point and a maximum of 10. A total of not less than 40 Green Star points is required to make up a champion and of the 40 points it is necessary to have four 5-point Green Stars awarded under four different judges, or two 5-Point and one Group win (value 10 points, under three different judges), or three 5- Point and one group win under four different judges. At least two Green Stars toward the title of champion must be gained after the dog reaches the age of 12 months.

In calculating the number of Green Star points won at any particular show, it should be noted that, if a dog wins Best of Breed over a bitch and the bitch has gained more points, the dog will benefit and obtain a higher number of points. The same applies to a bitch in similar circumstances. The rule awarding the Group winner a star equal in value to the highest awarded to any dog in the Group helps a really good dog in the less numerically strong breeds to gain its title.

Breed clubs

The Irish Dachshund Club in the South, affiliated to the Irish Kennel Club, and the Ulster Dachshund Club in the North, affiliated to The Kennel Club, are the only two breed clubs in Ireland. It is quite usual to belong to both clubs, and their history has been inter-twined over the years.

The Irish Dachshund Club was founded in 1932, and the Ulster Dachshund Club in 1946. Many founder members of the Ulster Club were already members of the Irish Dachshund Club. Mrs Marion Lysaght (née Moorehead), who is still very much with us, is a founder member of both clubs.

The Irish Dachshund Club today has a total membership of 168, and the Ulster Dachshund Club, 48. Sadly, the only show held under Kennel Club rules, the Belfast Championship Show, does not offer CCs to Dachshunds of any variety, so it is necessary for exhibitors to cross the Irish Sea to compete for them on mainland Britain. Conversely, there are 24 shows held under Irish Kennel Club rules offering Green Stars to all varieties of Dachshunds, and this seems to be very attractive to exhibitors who can, with luck and good entries, make up an Irish champion at as few as four Irish shows. This makes the competition keen, and the achievement of the Irish dogs who win at the top level all the more outstanding.

The show ring

The first champion in the breed was made up in Ireland in 1936. This was Ch/Ir Ch Red Card of Kelvindale, who also won in England, and was followed three years later by the first Wire champion, Ir Ch Sports Choreatium of Seton.

Dachshunds are very strong in Ireland, with breeders such as Mavis MacNaughton, whose von Grunparks blood lines trace back to Schwarenberg, Schneid and Luitpoldsheim. Then there is Rubie Hildebrand whose Longs were mainly Primrosepath breeding, and Peggy Seton-Buckley whose Seton Wires were based on Sports, and many other world famous blood lines. Lullie Huet added Silvae breeding to her Greygates Smooths and Seale to her Wires, and Peggy Rutledge imported Kyr von der Howitt, son of the famous Zeus, and Int Ch Ashdown Pirate to assist in maintaining the standard. Reading through the advertisements in the Irish Dachshund Club handbook published in 1945, one is struck by the number of outstanding Dachshunds in Ireland at that time. One kennel makes the boast: *This Kennel has sold so many dogs to England, all of which exhibited have won.* Perhaps the best two, however, are: *Kennels Established 1926. Renown for reliability, honest dealing, and first class stock... Has been sending stock to all parts of the world, but owing to the war, breeding is restricted. If impossible to breed the best, better not breed at all.*

Thanks to the high standards set by these and many other breeders, Dachshunds were well established in Ireland, and this was assisted by the Irish Kennel Club rule that permitted the crossing of coats. At this time Irish-bred Dachshunds were frequently shown on mainland Britain, with champions in all three coats on both sides of the Irish Sea.

Int Ch Greygates Tricket (Standard) shares a secret
with Greygates Mimi (Miniature).

Int Ch Greygates Slipper and
Int Ch Greygates Jive Dance:
Standard Wires bred by Mrs Lullie Huet.

In the last 10 years or more, only three kennels have made up Irish-bred champions under both British and Irish kennel club rules. We have Jennifer Cunningham with her Smooth Int Ch Celandine Catchfly and Joan and Lesley Patton with their Lesandnic Wires; British champions like Ch Lesandnic Lottabottle, Ch Lesandnic Sound of Music, Ch Lesandnic Snojoke, Ch Lesandnic In the Groove, Ch Lesandnic Salsabil, Ch Lesandnic Lucyrowe and Ch Lesandnic Logic. Then there is Ann Mathers, who bred Ch Metawand Tatu. An interesting point: the Lesandnic Wires on mainland Britain, all except one, go back to Greygates stock, and Lullie Huet also sent a Greygates Wire bitch to Jill Johnstone, where she became the foundation stock for the famous Silvae Wires.

Although the Miniatures varieties are the most popular, and British champions in all three coats have also been made up in Ireland, no Irish Miniature champion has yet achieved its crown in England. This is largely due to their absence from the show scene. Apart from at Crufts, and possibly one or two other shows, few exhibitors compete outside Ireland.

Some of the best known United Kingdom affixes feature in Irish pedigrees, but no dominant strain has yet emerged. This is possibly due to the practice of out-crossing, the taking of established lines to top winning dogs without enough thought to the compatibility of the pedigrees. To establish a dominant strain it is important to line breed in the first instance. Only when a certain type has become established should we think of out-crossing. I am therefore pleased to note that the earlier chapters in this book have endorsed this practice. Such a pity really when you consider that we still have the descendants from some famous lines. Delphiks are behind most of our Miniature Long-hairs, Dalegarth and Wingcrest also featuring strongly in Miniature Smooth pedigrees, and the importation of two Selwood Miniature Wires, who both became Irish Champions,

Int Ch Selwood Saminwha.   Ir Ch Selwood Catkin.

strongly influenced this variety with their bloodline for some years. In fact, the first Miniature Wire to achieve championship status in Ireland was Int Ch Selwood Saminwha.

Since Miniatures were recognised in Ireland they have become increasingly popular, and this has been at the cost of a falling-off of the Standard in all three coats. Very few, if any, breeders today own the large numbers of Dachshunds they once did, thus ensuring that there were always young dogs coming into the ring. With the loss of the 'big' names of the past, and the difficulty of obtaining really good stock from outside the country, there is a regrettable tendency for random breeding.

The strongest varieties are undoubtedly the Long-hairs, where careful selection and the importation of some already famous dogs from Britain have insured success at all levels in the show ring. Smooths and Wires have seen some well known affixes winning, but no kennel has emerged as an outstanding success story. The Miniature Long-hairs are strongest numerically, but the 'good' Miniatures are probably fairly evenly spread across all three varieties. The Ulster Dachshund Club runs two shows a year, both without tickets, and brings in specialist judges. The Irish Dachshund Club also runs two shows, one an Open Show at which new judges can gain experience, and the Championship Show in October each year where a Specialist judge from outside Ireland always officiates. These judges have consistently remarked on the high standard of many of the dogs shown, and have stated that the six finalists for Best in Show could hold their own at the same level at any Club in Britain. The other consistent observation, and one which is particularly pleasing, features the friendly and sporting atmosphere at our shows and the warm Irish welcome from all exhibitors.

All-breed championship shows in Ireland all take place between 17 March, when the show year starts with the Irish Club's St Patrick's Day Show, and the Dublin Dog Show Society's show on 27 December. All of them attract exhibitors from England, Scotland and Wales, with the greatest numbers coming in August for the Munster Circuit. There are group championship shows on the Saturdays prior to the start of the circuit, with shows at Clonmel, Killarney, Limerick and Tralee, giving the opportunity to attend five shows in eight days. As the entries are usually good, competitors have the chance to make up a champion in record time.

Pedigrees are fascinating to study and, although fashions change, those set in the past did so with much thought and a thorough knowledge of what lay behind the successful lines. The future success of Irish Dachshund breeding will depend on the way in which these lines, already present, are used in future breeding programmes. Careful line breeding with the use of good out-cross to complement what we have, the breeder keeping in mind the importance of soundness, temperament and quality rather than quantity, could ensure that the excellent foundations laid down by Irish Dachshund breeders in the past are not wasted.

United States of America

Dachshunds of all varieties took a massive beating during and immediately after the first World War in America: more, one might think, than in most English-speaking countries. The Dachshund became 'unpatriotic', to the extent that they changed the name to Badger Dog in an effort to preserve the breed. In 1923, the name Dachshund was restored. It is interesting to note that, in that year, the number of Dachshunds registered with The American Dachshund Club had fallen to an all-time low: just 26 dogs. But all was not lost. By the end of the 1930s these numbers had swelled to over 3000 a year.

Fortunately there were still a few staunch supporters of the breed throughout these trying times, foremost being Mrs C Davies Tainter with her Voewood Kennels. Present day Dachshund breeders in America owe her much credit for upholding not only the breed but also The Dachshund Club of America. Her foundation stock came from Semler, and among her best-known dogs were Ch Plum of West End and Ch Voewood Gizzie, later sold on to Mrs Justus Erhardt. Mrs Erhardt had the Teckelheim Kennels in Boston and Berlin, and it has to be said that Voewood had some very fine imports, many of which can still be traced to modern day pedigrees.

American readers will not need to be reminded of the many notable Dachshunds and enthusiasts who were responsible for the breed throughout their vast continent. Most American books have documented these names.

The Dachshund in America began with German and British imports and, while some were brought in from other countries, it was the German dogs that predominated. As with the British Dachshund, the breed in those early days was very much the preserve of the wealthy, who could afford to import good stock. Thankfully this is not the case today. Later on, the Dachshund's popularity was enhanced by notable and famous owners: they became fashionable. They were seen and photographed everywhere with people like Clark Gable, Adolphe Menjou, John Gilbert and Noel Coward. There was even a cartoon in the *Daily Mirror* depicting an adventurous and glamorous lady called Jane: with Fritz, her Dachshund, she became avid breakfast-time reading.

When the British and American Breed Standards are compared, it is interesting to note that the actual content differs very little apart from the wording. Perhaps it is worth quoting the section on colour, however, which does differ slightly from the British:

Color of Hair, Nose and Nails

(a) *One-colored Dachshund:* This group includes red (often called tan), red-yellow, yellow, and brindle, with or without a shading of interspersed black hairs. Nevertheless, a clean color is preferable, and red is to be considered more desirable than red-yellow or yellow. Dogs strongly shaded with interspersed black hairs belong to this class, and not to the other color groups. A small white spot is admissible but not desirable.

(b) *Two-colored Dachshund:* These comprise deep black, chocolate, gray (blue), and white; each with tan markings over the eyes, on the sides of the jaw and underlip, on the inner edge of the ear, front, breast, inside and behind the front legs, on the paws and around the anus, and from there to about one-third to one-half of the length of the tail on the underside. The most common two-colored Dachshund is usually called black-and-tan. A small white spot is admissible but not desired. Absence, undue prominence or extreme lightness of tan markings is undesirable. Nose and nails: In the case of black dogs, black; for chocolate, brown (the darker the better); for gray (blue) or white dogs, gray or even flesh color, but the last named color is not desirable; in the case of white dogs, black nose and nails are to be preferred.

(c) *Dappled Dachshund:* The color of the dappled Dachshund is a clear brownish or grayish color, or even a white ground,with irregular patches of dark gray, brown, red-yellow or black (large areas of one color nor desirable). It is to be desirable that neither the light nor the dark color should be predominate. Nose and nails: as for One- and Two-Colored Dachshund.

Our Ambassadors to the United States:
(left to right) Edna Cooper, Lovaine Coxon and Margaret Turner.

An American line-up, in which Miniatures and Standards are shown together.

Much of the information for this chapter was very kindly given to me by Margaret Turner who, along with two fortunate friends, Edna Cooper and Lovaine Coxon (see previous page), had the trip of a lifetime when they attended The Dachshund Club of America Centennial Show 1995. They were not the only British visitors: Jill Grosvenor-Workman of the Silvae affix with her companion Kim, Jeff Crawford of the Voryn affix, Lesley Patton of the Lesandnic affix and Elizabeth Medley and Ann Kennedy also attended.

Six American Clubs contributed to the Centennial Show, which lasted all of five days. It was held in a huge conference centre (I'm told it was three times the size of Picketts Lock in London) which was fully carpeted. American hospitality was outstanding: excellent hotel, swimming pool, sauna, jacuzzi and wonderful food. Margaret writes: 'I love American junk-food, they do it so well; it's gorgeous!'

I think perhaps I should get back to the matter in hand before we start sounding like a travel brochure. The reader will no doubt be interested in the comparisons. To begin with, the show started at 7.00 am. There were three main rings, large areas where each dog could really show off its movement. In the United Kingdom we have at least six rings, one for each variety and size. Unlike here, Standards and Miniatures are shown together, and the title given at each show may be worded differently.

Match shows, which are smaller and more informal and carry no points towards champion, accept puppies from three months onwards. The United Kingdom shows do not accept any dog less than six months of age on the day of the show to be exhibited or even to attend the show.

Then there are the licensed shows, Dachshund specialty, where exhibitors are able to earn an award of three to five points should they win. The speciality show, while it has more entries in the breed and in all varieties, usually has fewer overall entries than an all-breed event.

A chocolate dapple Standard Smooth, beautifully groomed for the ring.

The over-riding factor that impressed our visitors was the standard of preparation. All agreed it was superb. The dogs themselves also impressed them. There were minor differences on some points, but the consensus of opinion was that, overall, the Wires were outstanding – according to Margaret, they had to be seen to be believed.

It was also interesting in that the American show in general works on the points system. The Winner Dog, Winner Bitch and Best of Winners is based on the number of Dachshunds actually in competition. This system is not as confusing as one might initially think. Every show catalogue prints the American Kennel Club Scale of Points. These have to be counted accurately. The number of points is reflected in the number of Dachshunds present. These attendance numbers are counted from the judges list and the competitor may earn anywhere from one to five points (the most possible points at any one show).

Not only did our ambassadors bring back all the news from our American cousins, they also brought backsome very fine photographs. Unfortunately, not all of them were named. Rather I think, they were a lesson to demontrate our own somewhat conservative approach to colour (color) in our breed. Some of the colours, frankly, we have never seen anything like – particularly the piebald.

A special note: the term *yellow* as described in the American Breed Standards refers to what we call *cream*. Those confused by the description *piebald* should look at the photographs.

Overall the conformation of the Dachshund in America is outstanding and, when considering what lies beneath some of these somewhat 'technicolour' Dachshunds, we should not be too hasty or critical when denouncing them. After all, *all colours are permissible*.

Rather, perhaps, we should learn to accept that which is unusual with a more open mind.

Top two pictures: The standard of preparation in America was superb, as shown by this glamourous Long-hair and beautifully prepared Wire.
Bottom two pictures: An amazing range of colours was to be seen among the American exhibits.

Useful addresses

National Kennel Clubs

The Kennel Club
1–5 Clarges Street
Piccadilly
London   W1Y 8AB
Tel: 0171 629 5828

The American Kennel Club
Monday to Friday, 0830–1830 hours
(Eastern time)
Tel: 919 233 9767

Rescue Services

England
Valerie Skinner
Briarfields
Springfield Lane
High Green
Sheffield   S30 4JQ
Tel: 0114 2847425

Scotland
Iris Lashford
The Bungalow
Dysartmuir Farm
Kirkcaldy
Fife   KY1 3NY
Tel: 01592 882719

Weekly Canine Papers

Dog World
Somerfield House
Wotton Road
Ashford
Kent   TN23 6LW

Our Dogs
5 Oxford Road
Station Approach
Manchester   M60 1SX

Breed Clubs in the British Isles

The Dachshund Club
Hon Sec: Mrs P Hirst
Ehiwonnrn
Harford
Llanwrda
Dyfed   SA19 8DS
Tel: 01588 650428

The Irish Dachshund Club
Mrs Wendy Jackson
Bridge Cottage
Greenane
Rathdrum
Co Wicklow
Tel: 00353 404 46563

The Dachshund Club of Wales
Hon Sec: Mrs Brace
5 Clas Odyn
Whitchurch
Cardiff   CF4 1QF

The Scottish Dachshund Club
Hon Sec: Mrs J McNaughton
Balggownie
Ayr Rpad
Irvine
Ayrshire   KA11 5AB

Registered affixes

Approximately 50,000 affixes are currently registered with The Kennel Club, so you will understand that it would be a truly daunting task to name all the affix holders in the two sizes and six varieties of Dachshunds. We will do our best to name some of the more recent affixes in alphabetical order, and offer our sincere apologies to those reputable breeders we have missed. We also take this opportunity to remind readers that a full Affix Directory is available on request from The Kennel Club.

Abitibi . . . . Mrs L Lawrence-Starbuck
Abbalongdat . . . . Mrs A C Booth
Algiestone . . . . Mrs & Mr Batchelor
Amberliegh . . . . Mrs P Evans
Andlouis . . . . Mr & Mrs A Derry
Andyc . . . . Miss S M Raphael
Anousha . . . . Mrs & Mr Alcock
Antway . . . . Mrs H M Parker
Appydax . . . . Mr & Mrs Blackmore
Arietta . . . . Mrs J. Taylor
Ashridge . . . . .Mrs A Dunn
Auldmoor . . . . .Mr J Horswell
Aus-Bar . . .Mr, Mrs & Miss Koppenhaver

Balcombe . . . . Mrs J M Giacomelli
Barkesvale . . . . Mrs E M Stevens
Barlaine . . . . Mr & Mrs Mee
Barok . . . . Mrs M Edwards
Beltrim . . . . Mrs Cole-Hamilton
Bendigedig . . . . Mr & Mrs L Tavernor
Beralee . . . . Mr & Mrs Beardsley
Berrycourt . . . . Mr & Mrs Voaden
Bimini . . . . Miss Benson
Bokra . . . . Misses Surrell & Coleman
Bonnerhill . . . . . Mrs E Falconer-Douglas
Booth . . . . Mrs Foden
Boscolla . . . . Mr & Mrs Sainsbury
Bothlyn . . . . Mrs E Fulton
Bretarah . . . . Mrs E Morris
Brianolf . . . . Mrs F Winchurch

Bronia . . . . . Mrs Hannay & Mrs Mitchell
Brookmill . . . . Mrs J Pluck

Cairnsilk . . . . Mr & Mrs J Y Sinclair
Candover . . . . Mrs I Pain
Cedavoch . . Mrs J & Miss L McNaughton
Celandine . . . . Mrs J Cunningham
Chadrac . . . . Mrs C Hall
Chelane . . . . Mrs J Welton
Choefait . . . . Mrs J Lindstrom
Chorizo . . . . Mrs J Tabor
Christhausen . . . . Mrs B Bartlett
Claratan . . . . Mrs H Wildridge
Clarkevale . . . . Mr & Mrs Britten
Classidax . . . . Miss M Murphy
Clipperdown . . . . Mrs V Phillips
Coldenton . . . . Mr & Mrs G Clough
Cole Acre . . . . Mr & Mrs J H Wilson
Compudac . . . . Mr W L Giels
Conyer . . . . Miss S D Gatheral
Corrinbar . . . . Mr & Mrs Davis
Cotherstone . . . . Mrs A Morton
Cratloe . . . . Mrs E Fountain
Creekpit . . . . Mrs J Burge
Crewshound . . . . Mr & Mrs Pine
Cullerne . . . . Mrs V M Gibson

D'Arisca . . . . Mrs L Coxon
Dachsford . . . . Mr & Mrs Hardwick
Dachstown . . . . Mrs N Townsend

Dacshoe . . . . Mrs & Miss Keen
Dalanbeck . . . . . . Mr & Mrs J Goodman
Dalegarth . . . . Mr & Mrs Newbury
Damai . . . . Mrs A Sutton
Danbridge . . . . Mrs J Woolway
Dandydayo . . . . Mr D Roberts
Danverley . . . . Miss J Danvers
Danward . . . . Mrs D Edwards
Darsom . . . . Mrs C Dare
Daxmuir . . . . Mrs J Lashford
Daxvil . . . . Mrs P Lonnkvist
Deepfurrows . . . . Mrs S Moore
Denver . . . . Mr & Mrs Roberts
Devenwood . . . . Mrs P Anderson
Dianamo . . . . Mrs D Moate
Diggerman . . . . Mr & Mrs Gardner
Diminudax . . . . Mr & Mrs Brettell
Dizadak . . . . Mrs S Mundt
Djeata . . . . Mrs H Jamieson
Doubledax . . . . . Misses I Seidenbusch &
I Schulze
Drakesleat . . . . . . Mrs Z Thorn-Andrews
Dronwald . . . . Mr R Rowlands
Drydenlaw . . . . Mr & Mrs Bourhill

Elnside . . . . Mrs H McAulay
Emem . . . . Mrs M Dance
Evadanne . . . . Mrs A Hazelby
Eversweet . . . . Miss B Lambe

Fexionate . . . . Miss V Wood
Findowrie . . . . Mrs M Poole
Flavian . . . . Mrs K Laird
Foxbourne . . . . Mrs J Fox
Frankanswen . . . . Mrs W Barrow

Garrod . . . . Mr & Mrs H King
Garthorne . . . . Mrs A Callow
Gayteckels . . . . Miss D Abbott
Geffle . . . . Mrs J Forster
Gisbourne . . . . Mrs E Quick

Glasvey . . . . Mr W Warke
Glenrowan . . . . Mr & Mrs V Morris
Gottingen . . . . Mrs J Brittain
Graedon . . . . Mrs J Ireland
Guildway . . . . Mr & Mrs Bradbury

Halunke . . . . Mrs D Norton
Hampdach . . . . Mr & Mrs K Bethel
Hazelcroft . . . . Mrs G Thompson
Helenium . . . . Mrs H Buchan
Hobbithill . . . . Dr K Kershaw
Howrigg . . . . Mrs J Lamb
Huntford . . . . Mrs B Hutton

Imadac . . . . Mr & Mrs Earnshaw
Ingerdorm . . . . Mrs M Boulcott

Jadag . . . . Mrs D Graham
Janselgo . . . . Mrs G Makepeace
Jaydax . . . . Mrs J Atkinson
Jolival . . . . Mr & Mrs Hall
Jondac . . . . Mr & Mrs Widdop

Kantis . . . . Mr & Mrs A Atkins
Karinhall . . . . Mrs & Miss Herbert
Kershope . . . . Miss C Gatheral
Kireton . . . . Mrs & Miss Kerry
Kizzhar . . Mrs & Mrs M & Mr A Leighton
Knoxton . . . . Mrs S Gibb
Kyreburn . . . . Mrs G Hoskins

Landmark . . . . Mrs E Heeson
Lankelly . . . . Miss P Poulter
Larklinn . . . . Mr & Mrs J Thompson
Larrieux . . . . Mrs L James
Lesandnic . . . . Miss L J Patton
Loretto . . . . Mrs J Hallett

Malleda . . Mr & Mrs M & Mr A Leighton
Malynsa . . . . Mr & Mrs Marshall
Manakoora . . . . Mrs V Watkinson

Mardach	Mrs M Shankland
Marictur	Mrs M Turner
Maxred	Miss E Ingram
Maxwin	Mr & Mrs McLean
Maydays	Mr & Mrs Scott
Mazilba	Misses J M Bailey & E L Tyson
Meganhol	Mrs D Allam
Melriding	Mrs D Melbourne
Melvaley	Mr & Mrs J Burgin
Minard	Mr & Mrs Goddard
Minimead	Mrs G Mead
Montreux	Mrs A Negal
Morsefield	Mr & Mrs H Caple
Mouricia	Mrs P Seymour
Nevelder	Mr & Mrs Nordstrom
Nibelheim	Mr G Robinson
Nicholyev	Mr, Misses Bower
Northdax	Mrs J Ireland & Mrs B Diver
Pattaya	Mrs P Hancock
Peredur	Mrs R S Spong
Phaeland	Misses C L M & S D A Gatheral
Pickhill	Mrs J Naylor
Picklescott	Mrs D Clarke
Pipersvale	Mrs B Munt
Ploughland	Mrs G Ahrens
Ploughlands	Mr G Ahrens
Prudham	Mrs P Hampton
Quitrutec	Mr & Mrs Owen
Ralines	Mr & Mrs P Lockett & Mrs R Locket-Walters
Rarewood	Mrs C Woodhall
Regendachs	Mrs G M Raine
Rhodecot	Mrs M Hayman-Jeeves
Ritterburg	Mr & Mrs J Skinner
Rodima	Mrs & Miss Jordan
Roleta	Mr & Mrs Lovick-Gibbs
Romanchi	Mr & Mrs Moore
Rosanport	Mr & Mrs Goad
Rosenket	Mr & Mrs Rawson
Rugosa	Mrs D Fisher
Samlane	Mr & Mrs Price
Sandwells	Mrs M Sanders
Sanmik	Mr & Mrs Palin
Schon	Mmes A P Scherf & E Dorr
Scotmariner	Mrs M Miller
Shardagang	Mr & Mrs Blackburn-Bennett
Shardaroba	Mr & Mrs Bennet
Shelsue	Mrs & Miss Woods
Sierry	Mr J P Perry
Silkdown	Mr & Mrs Breese
Silvae	Mrs Grosvenor-Workman
Sonderwald	Mr & Mrs Holland
Sontag	Mrs E Cooper
Southcliff	Mr A Sharman
Springwood	Mrs B Walkey
Stargang	Helen Blackburn
Stoneferry	David & Clare Whalen
Sunara	Mrs Frazer-Gibson
Sunsong	Mr & Mrs Seath
Swanford	Mrs M Swann
Talberg	Mr & Mrs Diver
Tamaritan	Cdr M Belben
Tanska	Mrs B F Skanta
Tarchul	Mrs Pearson
Tarkotta	Mr & Mrs Pugh
Telmo	Mrs Entwistle
Terony	Mrs Winchurch
Toco	Mr L E Mitchell
Top Banana	Mr & Mrs Amano-Masaaki
Topthorne	Mrs M E Davies
Torella	Mrs & Miss Walker
Tuoela	Mrs Trimarco
Tythe	Mr & Mrs Williams